Valerie Vance Dillon

Becoming a Woman

Basic Information, Guidance & Attitudes on Sex for Girls

XXIII
TWENTY-THIRD PUBLICATIONS
Mystic, Connecticut
and
the columba press
Dublin, Ireland

Acknowledgment

The personal insights and professional medical knowledge of **Dr. Nancy Griffith, M.D.** were a valuable aid in the preparation of this book. She is a physician in family practice, with special interest in maternal and child care. In practice for 10 years, she is on staff at Henry County Memorial Hospital in New Castle, Indiana, and also works in the Maternal and Child Care Clinic of New Castle. Second oldest of 11 children, Dr. Griffith is a wife and mother of three. She and her dentist husband, Jim, have taught junior high sexuality courses and Pre-Cana for the engaged.

Fourth Printing 1995

Twenty-Third Publications
185 Willow Street
P.O. Box 180
Mystic, CT 06355
(203) 536-2611

ISBN 0-89622-433-3
Library of Congress Catalog Number 89-52154

The Columba Press
93 The Rise, Mount Merrion
Blackrock, Co Dublin
Ireland

ISBN 0-948183-84-5

"When I wrote *Becoming A Man* I was constantly urged to write a companion book for girls. I wisely resisted, saying that only a woman could do justice to a book entitled *Becoming A Woman*. I was glad I did. A woman—a wise and knowledgeable one—has fulfilled the task wonderfully.

"Valerie Dillon's book is the gracious work of a wife, mother of four daughters, worker in a Family Life Office, journalist, and Christian feminist. Colloquial and careful, this book treats the issues of female sexuality in an engaging and savvy way that will appeal to girls and young women of all backgrounds. It's a wise and warm book, insightful and delightful, one to be read by parents and put into the hands of their daughters. It's simply the best around—really terrific."

William J. Bausch

"Valerie Dillon's open approach to today's girls on issues relating to sexuality is refreshing and welcome. I especially commend the non-judgmental tone of this book, the inclusion of touchy areas like AIDS, the author's supportive invitation for today's girls to respect their own bodies and selves."

Dolores Curran, Columnist,
and author of *Traits of a Healthy Family*

"*Becoming a Woman* is presented with genuine Christian vision. It offers information on conception and sexual intercourse in the context of married love, the mystery and awesomeness of life before birth, and presents the family as a shaper of persons, both positively and negatively."

Ruth Charlesworth
Vermont Catholic Tribune

"...teaches a Christian sense of awe and respect for the body and human sexuality. Quite 'open' in explanation, generally moderate in definition and assumption."

Travis Du Priest
Living Church

"Communicating with teens and preteens is an art, and Valerie Dillon does it uncommonly well. She talks to girls about their sexuality in terms that are credible, down-to-earth, and faithful to the best of Catholic teaching.

"As young people grow up in an increasingly dangerous environment, they need help from adults who have credibility and can make a convincing case for sexual responsibility. (This book speaks to preteen and teenage girls about their sexuality in a relaxed and friendly tone, offering needed information and wise advice. Young readers will find affirmation, encouragement, and challenge here; their parents and teachers will get welcome assistance in the demanding task of sex education."

Rev. James DiGiacomo, S.J.

"A good book about a difficult topic, blending morality with an honest, open, and positive consideration of what it means to be a complete woman. Valerie Dillon is pleased and happy about being a woman, and she shares her enthusiasm with those who are privileged to read her book. Readers should include parents, who might be looking for an easy style of discussing sex with their daughters, and boys, who might learn to appreciate the beauty of womanhood more. I was captivated by the readable, straightforward approach."

James A. Kenny
Clinical Psychologist,

"Valerie Dillon writes at length about the challenges of growing up and the many choices that adolescent girls face in today's society. These choices include decisions on peer pressure, drug and alcohol use, and premarital sexual relations, with honest dialogue that explains the realities of each situation."

Mary Ann Wyand
The Criterion

Preface

In the early 1960s, when my four daughters were quite young, I co-authored a book with the late Walter Imbiorski, entitled *A Christian Guide to Your Child's Sex Life.* In the process, I learned almost as much as the girls did. Despite its (then) provocative title, *Your Child's Sex Life* was a simple, straightforward text, encouraging parents to recognize their primary role as educators and stressing that, from birth on, their children were sexual beings who learned about sexuality in myriad ways.

The need of young children, I said then, was for honest answers to questions, non-anxious responses to their curiosity, and positive modeling of what it is to be a man or a woman.

Much has changed in a quarter-century, both within the family and in society, but I believe that children's needs are still much the same. This is acutely so for teenagers, inundated as they are with false images of sexuality and its meaning.

Today's adolescents need information, personal insight, and value-based guidance at much younger ages than they once did. Not only are they entering puberty earlier, but they are maturing sexually in a culture that has swung, like a pendulum, from negative and puritanical silence to obsessive preoccupation with sex in all its aberrant forms.

In the 1960s many of us objected to sex education in most school settings, believing that it usurped the parental role. Now, it seems apparent that conscientious adults, especially within the religious sector, can assist parents as they guide their sons and daughters toward a wholesome and Christian understanding of what it is to be sexual persons.

Becoming a Woman is written in the hope that young people, their parents, and other adults who care about youth will find it an honest, practical, and helpful book. It is not targeted for adults (though they most certainly are encouraged to read it). Rather, it is for and about girls between 10 and 15 years of age, and is intended to serve as a companion volume to Rev. William Bausch's work, *Becoming a Man* (Twenty-Third Publications).

We hope that, together, these books can enable our young men and women to better appreciate and honor their God-given gift of sexuality.

To the Young Teen,

Growing up in today's world is no snap. Exciting—yes. Easy—no way. Because you live in a time of great change and confusion, of freedom and virtually unlimited choices, it's sometimes hard to be a loving, moral person these days. There isn't always adult support and example for you.

If you are a young teen, a person on the threshhold of womanhood, this book is for you. If you are searching for some answers to life and its meaning and your place in it, you may discover some of those answers here.

If you are confused about the changes in your body as well as in your spirit, you will find reassurance and guidance in what follows. If sexual issues concern you, this book offers help. If you are struggling to grow up and there's the nagging question of "Who, really, am I?"—you may find hope and some clues within these pages.

Becoming a Woman is written with you, the young teenager, in mind. If offers facts and information, suggestions and stories. Its goal is to help you grow in appreciation of yourself as a sexed person.

Although it is especially for you, there also are some words for your parents, who love you and who want to help you as you move toward adulthood. My hope is for deeper sharing and honest communication between you and your family as you mature. Use this book, if you can, to further such dialogue.

Good reading and blessings to you!

Dedicated to the memory of my mother
Rose Vance,
my best role model,
whose nurture gave me roots,
whose daring gave me wings

Contents

Part Three
Who I Choose to Be

Part One

Who I Am

1~

The World According to Me

Once upon a time, there was a girl—let's call her Stephanie—who looked forward to becoming a woman. She was a young teenager and she had an older sister, Julie, who was 17, and she envied the fun her sister had.

Stephanie wasn't exactly pretty but she was pleasant looking with wavy brown hair and blue eyes, and she was friendly, liked cats and funny stories, and worked hard at school. She day-dreamed a lot and wrote in a diary she hid from her family, and—on good days—could hardly wait for the time that she would go out on dates.

Sometimes Stephanie felt very self-conscious and unsure of herself. Although she had girlfriends, she wondered at times if they really liked her. In class, she got flustered and embarrassed when the teacher called on her for an answer. As for boys, once she had thought they were pests, but lately she found them rather exciting and there was one boy that she especially liked.

Stephanie could be anyone. She could be lots of girls. She could be you.

If you are between 10 and 15 and on the verge of growing up, you are in the most exciting, confusing, scary, fun time of life: adolescence! It's a time of transition when you change emotionally, mentally, and physically, when you begin to mature sexually. And when this period is over, you will emerge from it as a new, unique, and mature young adult woman.

Yet, in a mysterious way, you always will remain *you*! Your genetic makeup, passed on from parents, grandparents, and other relatives before them, stays with you forever. You will always have the same-shaped nose, the length of legs in proportion to your body, the same color hair (unless you decide to help it out!), the same tone of voice, basic temperament, and above all, the same gender: female.

I hope you think being a female is wonderful. It's your way of *being* to the world and to all the people you care about. Sexuality really is a gift from God. The purpose of this book is to encourage you to rejoice in becoming a woman. I also hope it will help you better understand boys and how to deal with sexual issues during your teen years.

Back, for a minute, to the person you are today. If you were asked to write a description of yourself, what would you say? A physical description might be the easiest thing: height, weight, color of hair, length of eyelashes, color of eyes and skin, your facial features (some very nice, some so-so).

But how would you describe your inner self? The feelings you have about life? How would you explain the thoughts you think, the dreams you dream, the warm feelings you get at Christmas, the prayers you whisper that only God can understand?

No doubt of it, you are a mystery, a unique, one-of-a-kind person who will never be duplicated. The question is: what do you think of this person? Would you describe yourself as smart? Quiet? Quick witted? Kind? Easy-going? Hot-tempered? Enthusiastic? Sexy? Sentimental?

More important, how well do you like yourself? Do you love yourself? I hope you love yourself. When our Lord Jesus was walking on this earth, he told people they should love others *as they loved themselves*. He reminded them that God his Father (and ours too) made each person in the divine image. Every one of us has a spark of God's life in us. Somehow, though not physically, we resemble God. You can figure out from this why Jesus knows we will love ourselves: God made us, and as they say, God doesn't make junk!

So now what do you think of yourself? How's your self-esteem? If you don't believe you're good and lovable and worthwhile, you're missing the message Jesus wants you to hear. And, this is important, you're making it hard to grow into a happy, mature, and sexual Christian.

There's a connection, you see, between loving yourself and being a loving person. If you don't like yourself, you're going to find it hard to like others just for themselves. Instead, you'll spend most of your time trying to impress other people just so you can feel good about yourself. You'll want them to keep reassuring you that you're okay, because you don't have that feeling inside yourself. And when you depend on others for self-love, sometimes you do things to win their approval, even though it may mean going against your own beliefs. Then you think less of yourself, and your love for others becomes even more self-centered.

Some girls tell me it's hard to like themselves during these teen years. They feel so mixed up and unsure of themselves. You might agree. Some days, you do what you should, but other days you don't. Maybe you're mean to your little brother or you're fresh with your Mom or fail a test. Then you feel guilty and you don't like yourself very much. That kind of guilt is okay because it helps you to decide to be better, to try harder.

One young girl I know put it this way: "Sometimes, I don't even know myself: I act in ways that aren't like me at all. I don't know what gets into me. And I feel bad about it."

If those are some of your feelings too, welcome to the human race! All of us on occasion do things we know are wrong. Welcome to adolescence, when roller-coaster emotions and behavior are typical of these years. The unexpected bad moods, the strong emotions, the fantastic highs, sometimes horrible embarrassment—all are feelings you have to deal with.

If you've always been a patient, loving, and obedient daughter, it's hard to understand (both for you and your parents) when you turn crabby, sneaky, or sharp-tongued.

For much of this, blame the changes in your body and mind that are creating turmoil. It won't always be this way. For now, you need to know that you're still a good and loving person. You might say to yourself each morning: Be patient. God isn't finished with me yet!

Questions for Reflection/Discussion

1. What makes you unique? What are some things that will always be a part of you, no matter how old you are?

2. How do you feel about being female? When do you especially like being a girl?

3. What is the best part of becoming a teenager? What, so far, are the biggest challenges?

2~

How I Got to Where I Am

Knowing where we come from helps us to understand who we are. The story of how you came into existence is a fascinating one. You may know parts of it: what your parents told you about your earliest days as a baby. But for each of us the real beginning goes back a good bit before birth. It goes back to when parents made marriage vows to each other, promising to love one another and be together for all their days. They had sufficient love and trust and faith in themselves and each other to publicly make these promises before family and friends and their church.

Such a marriage creates a unity, a oneness in two people that wasn't there before. Not only does the couple merge their living quarters, their interests, and their bank accounts, but, more important, they merge their lives emotionally, spiritually, and physically.

Ideally, they become responsible for each other's wellbeing, encouraging one another when bad days come, sharing the joy and fun of good days, the misery and heartache of bad ones. They pray together for the courage and wisdom to live as good Christians. And they hope to share their love and life with children. They become what the Bible calls "two in one flesh."

There's a special physical relationship that God intends only for married couples to share. You know that when you care about someone, you want to be close to them. You enjoy a hug or kiss, a playful pat or even just a handshake with someone you like. For married couples, though, physical affection goes beyond this to a more intimate and complete expression of love, called marital, or sexual, intercourse. The man places his erect penis into the woman's vagina and a "climax" is reached—ejaculation and intense feelings of release and pleasure.

This act of love serves three purposes: (1) It allows the wife and husband to express their feelings in a deeply pleasurable way. (2) It helps them build love and deepen their bonds. (3) It gives them power to share with God in the creation of a new human life.

When marital union, or intercourse, takes place, male semen, containing sperm, passes from the man's into the woman's body. If this enters an egg cell present in the woman, conception takes place.

And so it was with you. This was when your life began: at conception, after your parents' act of sexual intercourse. When the egg from your mother merged with the sperm from your father, the single fertilized cell (which was you) contained 46 matched chromosomes—23 each from your Mom and Dad. At that moment, your most basic identity was formed!

The chromosomes contained genes, hundreds of them, which you inherited from your parents, your grandparents, and all your ancestors before them. These genes combined by chance from thousands of possible combinations and made you different from everyone else in the world.

You are unique! There never has been anyone before you

with exactly your bodily traits, personal characteristics, and natural talents.

Your sex, your rate of growth, the color of your eyes, your skin and hair, the eventual length of your nose and fingers and toes, your basic emotional makeup, your predisposition to certain diseases, whether you have artistic talent or sing off-key, your intelligence potential—all of these and many more factors were decided at conception.

How your sex was determined is different from other hereditary factors. It involves sex chromosomes, with X being the female chromosome. The mother always contributes an X chromosome, but the father's sperm might contain either an X or a Y. If a Y sperm fertilizes the egg, the child will be a boy. In your case, you got an X from both parents. So, you can thank your Dad for contributing that second X, causing you to be born female!

Questions for Reflection/Discussion

1. What specific traits have you inherited from your mother's side? From your father's?

2. What is your reaction to this chapter's explanation of sexual intercourse? Did you learn anything new or helpful? What?

3. Think of some facts and ideas concerning sexuality that you learned from your parents. Were these learned from their words, their attitudes, or their actions?

~3

My Life in the Womb

The story of your first months of life is indeed a fantastic one. During the first week after conception, the fertilized egg that was you traveled down the fallopian tube into your mother's uterus, or womb, all the while dividing and subdividing into many cells. It then burrowed into the lining of the womb. And there you grew until you were ready to be born.

By the time you were four weeks old, you had the barest beginnings of eyes, a spinal cord, nervous system, thyroid gland, lungs, stomach, liver, kidney, intestines. The first faltering beats of your heart had begun. Your arms and legs had started to bud. And you were only one-fifth of an inch long!

By eight weeks, you had all of your internal organs, a little mouth with lips and a tongue, and buds for 20 milk (baby) teeth. There was readable electrical activity of your brain through an EEG. And you had begun to resemble a fantastically tiny human baby, though you were not more than an inch in length! You now were called a fetus.

By about 12 weeks, your permanent skeleton of bone had replaced the cartilage; the first layers of your skin appeared. Your heart was the size of a pea, and it vigorously pumped blood through super-fine veins. No larger than your father's thumb, you already were organically complete and fully formed.

Maybe you don't like swimming now, but by the time you were 16 weeks, you floated freely, weightlessly, and gracefully in the water-filled amniotic sac which protected you from injury. Your tiny arms and legs thrashed randomly about, touching, feeling, and exploring your world. At times, you got tangled up in your umbilical cord, a lifeline through which food and waste traveled between yourself and your mother.

Your fingernails were just beginning to grow and you might have scratched yourself as you moved your arms about. In fact, you may have needed your first manicure immediately after birth. Ask your mother!

As you floated free in the sac (bag of water), you sucked and swallowed small amounts of fluid, learning these skills for that exciting day after birth when you had to suck and swallow if you were going to survive (obviously you did). Some time during this early stage, your little mouth encountered your thumb—and you sucked it!

Your eyes were sealed shut to protect them from infection and you already had eyelashes. You now measured about 5.5 inches and weighed only 6 ounces! Although you were very active, your mother probably couldn't yet feel you moving.

By 20 weeks, you had the markings through which you can always be identified, even today: your fingerprints!

You may think you have sharp hearing now, but in the womb your hearing was already acute. You listened and even responded to the noises outside of you: your mother's body, her heartbeat, the growling of her empty stomach when she resisted a late-night pizza. You even heard noises from the world outside: a car horn, the alarm clock, your father yelling at a brother or sister you hadn't yet seen. If the noise was loud and sudden, you instinctively jumped.

During the last three months, there was little new development. Instead, you grew plumper and stronger, adding about five pounds by the time of birth. Your skin was less wrinkled and began to thicken. Your legs, much like an ape's, were shorter than your arms. By the ninth month all your organs were prepared to function on their own. In short, you were ready for life in the outside world just 38 weeks or so after that miraculous moment of conception when your parents and God called you into being. From that original first cell, by the time of birth you had grown into a staggering total of some 200 million differentiated cells!

But your mother and father would have been furious if anyone had described you that way. To them, you were an absolutely beautiful creature, even if your skin was red and the top of your head had a soft spot and you cried loudly every single night between 6:00 and 9:00.

From birth on, you continued to grow at an incredible rate, doubling your birth weight by six months of age. You learned to crawl, then walk in the first year or so (ask your folks when that first step took place). Because the family loved you and thought you were the cutest baby ever, they cooed and cuddled you, babbled at you as they changed your diaper, sang and rocked you, fed you, took you for walks. Before long, you began to say words, then sentences. When you began to ask questions, you probably drove everyone crazy. Most important, you learned to know that other people would be there when you needed them.

The "terrible twos" arrived and you learned the word "no" and used it as often as possible. This was normal. It happens when a little tyke discovers she's a separate person and wants to control as much as she can of her little corner of the world.

You learned all sorts of things in your first five years, and before long, it was time to enter school. Do you remember your first day of kindergarten or first grade? My oldest daughter, Karen, still reminds me that I put her on the high school bus her very first day! I was too nervous and excited to notice the other kids were three times her size! Maybe your mother or father remember their feelings too when their little girl stepped out into the big world, never again to belong only to them.

Questions for Reflection/Discussion

1. What is your reaction to the description of life in the womb? Which details did you like best? Why? What surprised you?

2. What was your "birth story?" Where and how were you born? What was your weight and height? How much hair did you have? Did you look "funny?"

3. Think back and remember your earliest memory from childhood. What does it mean to you today? Why do you remember it?

~ 4

My Family: How It Shapes Me

If you want to really understand yourself, understand your family! This might mean your mother and father and a brother, or a houseful of kids and just Mom, or parents and a grandmother and just you. Today, families come in all sizes and shapes. Families are now more diverse in our country than at any other time. More than anything else in your life, your family influences how you turn out. The reason is simple. From your earliest days, family members passed on their ideas, their beliefs, their love, and all sorts of encouragement and support. Ideally, they:

- Applauded as you taught yourself to turn over in your crib, to hold a rattle tight, to crawl, feed yourself, walk, tie your shoes, fly a kite, and to learn a thousand other complicated skills. You blossomed with the help of this support and attention.
- Taught you right from wrong, acceptable behavior from unacceptable. And because you loved them, you wanted to do what was right and to earn their approval.

• Helped you to understand other people's needs and wants. They reminded you that your little brother needed your help, that Dad was tired and wanted some quiet, that Grandma should receive a thank you note from you for your birthday present.

• Shared their beliefs about God and gave you their own example of faith and prayer. You learned from your family that you could reach out to God when you were troubled, and God would hear you and in some way answer your prayer.

• By word and example passed on family values about how to live, work, celebrate, forgive, spend money, and be a woman. They communicated other attitudes and beliefs that are deeply ingrained in you, even though you may hardly be aware of them.

As you grow up, you probably will challenge some of these values. You may argue about the wisdom of parental rules. This is pretty normal, a way for you to form your own values. But even if you reject family beliefs, you probably will find yourself moving back to many of them as you reach adult life, marry, and begin your own family.

A very significant way your family influenced you is in sexual roles. You are a girl; you know that. But what does it mean to be a girl? Maybe in your family it meant playing with dolls and housekeeping toys, wearing frilly dresses, taking dancing lessons, and being a sweet, smiling charmer.

Maybe your family specializes in "tomboys" who play ball, climb trees, and follow big brothers. Or maybe the girls in your family are encouraged just to be who they are, with a mix of so-called feminine and masculine traits.

Do you know what a "stereotype" is? In sexual terms, it's a very narrow, limited way of looking at a specific person. It's a label that says if you're a girl, you are expected to behave, think, act in a particular way. Stereotypes have faded in many families, which allows boys and girls greater freedom to develop their unique personalities. This is healthy and good.

Of all that your family has given you, by far the most important thing has been love, for love is the one absolute necessity for human beings. Did you know that without love, you would die emotionally and even physically? God made us this way, creating us out of love and putting this drive in us to love others and be loved back.

Some years ago in a large East Coast hospital, the babies in the nursery all stopped eating, cried a lot, and acted sick. The doctors could find nothing physically wrong, but the babies definitely were not well. It was feared they might die. Finally, an old nurse made a suggestion: Let's give the little ones more attention; let's play music in the nursery. Let's hold them while they take their bottle and talk to them when we change their diaper. They need more attention and affection. She was right! With more loving care, those babies became healthy again!

Like them, you would have died as a baby without people around to care for you, hold you, coo at you, and let you know how important you were. By their attention and affection, your family helped you to understand that you mattered, that you were lovable and valuable.

The fact that you now are nearly grown doesn't at all stop your desire to be loved. Adults, too (including your parents), need to feel that others care for them. Like babies and you, they also crave affection, touching, and loving care.

This need for love is built into our human nature. We thrive physically and psychologically only when we have enough of it. Of course, the way that love is expressed depends on the relationship, whether it is between mother and child, father and mother, girlfriend and girlfriend, or girlfriend and boyfriend.

And, of course, as you reach teenage years, big hugs and kisses from Dad, holding hands with Mom may no longer suit you. At various stages of life, love needs to be expressed in appropriate ways.

If I asked you right now to make out a list of all the

things your family has done and been for you, you might be surprised. Even though you sometimes quarrel with your brother or resent your big sister or feel angry at your mother because she scolded you, deep down you know that the members of your family are very important to you. You can't imagine life without them.

Questions for Reflection/Discussion

1. What do you like most about your family? Are there any things you would like to change?

2. Who has influenced you most in your life? What beliefs and values has this person given you?

3. Does your family have a strong opinion about the "ideal girl"? Did they expect you to conform to that image? Did you?

4. Reflect on the women in your family—your mother, grandmothers, aunts, older sisters, etc. How would you describe them? Do you want to be like any (all) of them?

~ 5

Bad Things Happen to Good People

No family is perfect, and in some families serious things go wrong that affect the healthy growth of all members. Let's look at some examples:

Margo grew up in a home where father's word was law. No one was permitted to argue with any rule or demand he made, and if her mother tried to take Margo's side, she was angrily silenced.

The problem was that Margo's father had grown up in a family where his father was boss; in fact, he used the strap on his children to make them behave. As is often the case, Margo's father became the same kind of parent. He believed that he alone had the right answers, and his favorite saying was "Children are to be seen and not heard!"

Margo and her brothers and sisters lived in fear of displeasing their father because he would ridicule and shame them in front of their friends or make them stay home for a week, no matter how minor the misbehavior. It wasn't that he was a bad man; it was his upbringing. He learned to be a parent from his own father who was a harsh man. Margo also may learn to be like her father, but more likely she will pattern herself after her mother, a passive and frightened woman. Margo may even marry a strict, authoritarian man like her father because that is what she has grown used to.

As she reached high school, Margo was a lonely and unhappy girl with a poor image of herself as a young woman. Fathers usually are the first signs to young girls whether they are attractive and lovable. In Margo's case, she got an opposite message from her father. She felt unlovable and ugly, so she kept to herself and her sexual maturing was painful for her.

Margo's classmate, Hannah, is an only child and her mother and father are divorced. Hannah lives with her Mom, but sees her Dad every weekend. She has never told her parents, but she believes she is the reason why their marriage broke up. She used to hear them fighting over her, arguing over rules, her clothes, her friends, how to discipline her, how to keep her "out of trouble." Hannah finally decided that if it weren't for her, her folks would still be married. And it makes her feel sad and very guilty.

Even worse, Hannah's parents still use their daughter to wage war. When she goes out with her father, she hears all the bad things about her mother that made her father mad. He asks questions about her mother's activities and friends. Her mother does the same thing, warning Hannah before her father picks her up that he had better set a good example, better than when he lived at home. She repeatedly asks Hannah if her father has ever brought a woman with them on their outings.

Hannah feels like a football in the middle of a deadly game. Tense and nervous as each weekend approaches, she is beginning to have problems sleeping and her school grades have slipped badly. In spite of it all, Hannah loves both her parents and wishes they could all be a family together again. However, she is not sure she ever wants to fall in love and marry because she can see the hurt it can bring.

Terry, 11, lives in an alcoholic home. Her mother, though few people know it, drinks too much. Every day Terry comes home from school, afraid that she will find her mother drunk in bed and her younger sister and brother running wild around the house.

Terry's Dad is a sales representative who travels a lot and somehow he doesn't seem to know how bad things are in the house. Terry doesn't want to say anything against her mother, so when her father returns she pretends everything is fine.

As the oldest child, she "covers" for Mom and tries to take care of her younger sister and brother. In fact, her grandmother calls her "the little mother." Terry often fixes dinner, scrambling eggs or warming TV meals in the microwave. She makes sure the younger kids get their homework done and go to bed on time. Later, she tries to get her mother to eat something. Finally, Terry gets to her own homework.

Terry's mother keeps promising she will go to parent's night at school, to pick her up after late assembly, to take the children to a movie. But she never does. Many times, Terry's mother has promised she will stop drinking, but she doesn't. She promises every morning that things are going to get better, but they never do. And now Terry has begun to lose her confidence in people. She believes she must "go it alone" and tell no one because people can't be trusted.

Once a friendly, outgoing girl with lots of friends, Terry no longer brings girlfriends to the house. She's afraid to be embarrassed. She loves her mother dearly and lies to others and herself about what is really going on. Deep down, though, Terry is ashamed and angry and frightened, but she can't admit these feelings. She wonders if her father feels the same way.

Tanya's problem is even more desperate. She was sexually abused by her uncle, her mother's brother. It started a year ago when she was 11 and Uncle Willie would babysit her. When he hugged and touched her, she felt strange and bad about it but said nothing. After all, he was her uncle. Then, one night, she woke up and found him in bed with her and he forced her to have sex with him. He told her, "This is just a way to show I love my little niece."

It has happened several times since. Tanya knows it is wrong and she must tell her mother. But she feels so guilty and ashamed, as though, somehow, she is responsible. She's afraid her mother will blame her. And she keeps wondering what she did to cause this bad thing to happen.

Tanya told a teacher at school but later acted like it was all made up when the teacher said she would have to report her story to the authorities. Tanya is terrified that the police will come and take her away, or maybe her uncle. She's afraid her mother won't love her any more. Worst of all, she is beginning to have pleasurable feelings when her uncle does it to her.

What kind of a girl could she be? She is rotten, that's what she thinks. Poor Tanya needs protection and loving help or she will grow up with deep guilt and twisted ideas about sex and about herself as a woman.

Such family situations are real, and children often are the biggest victims. But adults usually don't deliberately hurt their children—not if they are sane. Family members who harm a young child don't intend to inflict pain or cause emotional damage. The problem often is that they were abused themselves as children, and, without wishing to, they do the same when they become adults.

What is terrible about such situations is that the children they harm carry their own wounds and memories into adulthood. And as they struggle to love and be loved, they never quite get over feeling ashamed, inadequate, and unlovable.

Families in crisis need assistance from outside the home.

There are many people who can help: doctors, priests, counselors, self-help groups for alcohol and drug abusers, divorced people, etc.

If the family fails to seek help, children need to find a trustworthy person such as a teacher, a school counselor, a priest or religious sister or brother and tell their story. Otherwise, the pain and hurt may last a long time and may even be passed from your generation to the next.

If you know of someone—or *you are* that someone—don't be afraid to seek help. There are people who will believe you and who will try to find you the help that you and your family need.

Questions for Reflection/Discussion

1. How and where did you learn about sex? In what ways has this shaped your attitude toward being a sexual person?

2. If there are family problems, who can you go to for help? Do you? Does your family talk about its problems and work together to solve them? How?

3. How would you describe your family to a stranger?

6~ Time for Questions

Q: How often do married people have sex?

A: It really depends on the couple. There's no such thing as a normal number of times. Some married people have sexual intercourse several times a week; others once or twice a month. It depends on the couple's physical and emotional makeup, their lifestyle, their sex drive, and other factors.

Q: I'm the only one in eighth grade who's not wearing a bra yet. I'm absolutely flat! Is there something wrong with me?

A: Nothing that a little time won't cure. Remember, you've got your own timetable; you'll develop according to your own biological clock. Remember, no one but you is so conscious of your shape. Instead of worrying, concentrate on being a fun person and be confident that changes are coming soon.

Q: My parents won't tell me, but I'm sure I'm adopted. I don't look anything like anyone else in the family. How can I find out for sure?

A: Looks don't prove a thing. Think of all of the people who came before you in your family, and all of the possible physical traits you could get from them! You could look like a thousand different people. But you sound like you might have other reasons for thinking you're adopted. Ask for a serious talk with Mom or Dad (or both), and put the question to them. Tell them you're old enough to know. Believe what they tell you. One of my daughters had the same doubts; it's not uncommon at your age.

Q: There's liquor around our house and lately, I've started to help myself to it when no one's around. Does this mean I'm an alcoholic?

A: It might mean you're just curious about the effects of alcohol; lots of kids are. But it also might be the beginning of a problem. Alcoholism runs in families. It's a disease that strikes quickly, especially people who have what we call a predisposition to alcoholism. Don't risk it. Stop drinking right now. There may be trouble ahead if you don't. And if you sneak behind your family's back, eventually your folks will lose their trust in you, and with good reason.

Q: My folks fight all the time. It really upsets me. Can I do anything to get them to stop?

A: First, don't take sides; stay out of the argument itself. Second, tell each of them how much it hurts you and how scared you get when they quarrel. Ask them, for your sake if not theirs, if they would be willing to go to a marriage counselor. And let them know you love them.

Q: I'm scared to start high school. My folks are making me go to the Catholic school and I don't know anyone there. Why can't they understand how I feel?

A: Have you told them? You'll feel better if you express your fears, even if they don't change their mind about the school. But all freshmen worry about making friends, about fitting in, about finding their way around and learning the routine at a new, bigger school. In your first few days, look for someone who's alone like you, then introduce yourself. It may not be the beginning of a long friendship, but it will help you get over the jitters. Keep busy, work hard on your studies, be friendly, and before you know it, you'll belong!

Q: My sister had a miscarriage. Is that the same as an abortion?

A: Oh, no. Doctors may call it a "spontaneous abortion," but it's not the same thing as causing the baby to die. Miscarriage is when an unborn infant is naturally expelled from the mother's body before it's able to survive. Usually, this happens in the first few months and may occur because the baby isn't developing normally. It's no one's fault, but it can make parents very sad.

Q: If there are so many sperm, how come only one child is conceived?

A: There's normally only one mature egg present in the woman's body. The first sperm that penetrates the egg fertilizes it. All the others wither and die soon after.

Q: What causes twins?

A: There are two kinds of twins: fraternal and identical. Fraternal twins happen if a woman releases two eggs at nearly the same time and each one is fertilized by a different sperm from the father. Fraternal twins may be of the same or opposite gender. They do not look any more alike than other brothers or sisters. They have different sets of genes. Identical twins are more unusual, developing when the fertilized egg splits in two soon after conception. In this case, the two babies will have identical genes, so that they not only strongly resemble each other but may even have similar temperaments and grow up to be very close psychologically. Of course, they will always be the same sex.

Q: Why do parents want a lot of kids? I don't want more than one.

A: Not all parents do, but some love having three or four or more kids around them. They think it's a lot of fun to have a big family, even though they know it's also a lot of work. Families used to be bigger when they lived in big old houses or on the farm where the kids could help out. But today, it's not so easy to take care of a large family. Education and housing costs much more and, unfortunately, our society doesn't appreciate large families as it used to.

Q: My mother embarrasses me when I bring my friends home. She asks them questions and won't leave us alone. How can I get her to understand that she's not one of us?

A: She may be trying to decide what kind of friends you're making. Or she might just want to be friendly. Thank her for that, and as kindly as you can, tell her you'd appreciate it if she didn't ask too many questions or hang around too long. Don't be surprised if she says she wants to know they're the right kind of kids. Parents worry about this. Also, realize that it's hard for parents who've been close to their children to let go of those close bonds.

Q: I can't get any privacy in my house. My sister and brothers, even my parents, are constantly walking into my room. Can't they respect my right to be left alone?

A: They may not realize that, as you grow up, you need private space to just be alone. If your door is shut, no one should walk in on you without knocking and waiting for a reply. In a nice way, explain how you feel and ask your mother for a house rule that respects everyone's privacy.

Q: This is my Mom's second marriage, and I *hate* my stepfather. He isn't my father, and I resent it when he acts like he can boss me around. What gives him the right?

A: He's probably as scared as you about this new relationship and he may be trying too hard. Could you tell him, in a kind way, that you don't want him to try to replace your father? No doubt, you still love and miss your Dad. That's normal. But your Mom needs you to try to get along with her new husband, for their sake as well as yours. Be patient, and be honest enough to admit his good points.

Q: I really hate myself. I'm a mess. I have ugly hair and a terrible face, no shape. I don't even like my personality. What hope is there that I'll ever have friends in high school?

A: Whoa! You sound like you're at what we used to call "the awkward age." That's when you're between little-kid cuteness and the neat good looks of a young woman. The question is: what can you do for yourself right now? You can start by knowing that there's lots of beauty *inside* that may not be showing on the outside because you feel so bad about yourself. Let that good stuff—kindness, humor, concern for others, determination, a sense of fun, etc.—come out to shine! Ask your parents or a good friend what they like about you and then *believe* their answers.

At the same time, work on your appearance. Get a different hairstyle—something new and sharp. See a druggist or a doctor about something to improve your skin. Be sure to get enough sleep. Diet *only* if you need to. And be patient with this growing-up stage. Better times are ahead.

Q: They always tell you to "love yourself" in religion class. That's hard for me. I've done some really bad things and I know God's going to punish me. If my folks knew what I did, they wouldn't love me any more.

A: All of us have done "bad things" of one kind or another. You sound like you're really sorry and that's a big step. If you're Catholic, go to confession to a priest—that's a formal church way of seeking forgiveness. Tell Jesus of your sorrow for whatever you've done, and if you can make amends for the "bad things," do it now. Just remember that God forgives us and wants us to forgive ourselves for our sins. An important step is to learn from your mistake and to start over again with new courage. Don't give up on yourself. God hasn't.

Part Two

What I Am Becoming

7~ The Wonder of My Body

Every person has her or his own timetable for reaching sexual maturity. But on the average, girls mature two or three years sooner than boys and may begin as early as 9 or 10—or as late as 15. The average age probably is about 12.

If you're not already in puberty (the name for sexual maturing), how can you tell if it's coming? First, there's a surge in physical size: your skirts and jeans seem to shrink every time they're washed. Your blouses begin to seem snug. You're shocked to discover you tower over your best friend when you used to be the same height. You worry that you'll become a giant!

After physical growth comes the development of what biologists call secondary sex characteristics. Often, for girls, the first is breast development, and this is an exciting, if somewhat embarrassing, occurrence. Occasionally, one breast develops faster than the other and a girl worries that something is wrong. But if this happens to you, there's nothing to worry about; the size of the breasts will eventually even up. Another feminine thing happens in puberty: the hips broaden to make you physically able some day to carry and give birth to a baby.

Also, hair appears in the genital area and, later, on the arms and legs and under the arms. You begin to notice perspiration odor, requiring daily use of a deodorant. Sweat glands have become more active and increased oil on the skin may cause pimples and other blemishes. It's a time when scrupulous cleanliness and gentle care of your skin will minimize complexion problems.

The most dramatic sign of sexual maturation is menstruation, a normal function for mature girls and women. In menstruation, the bloody lining of the uterus is passed out of the body through the vaginal opening. Menstruation is a sign that your body is preparing itself for the ability to have children.

Your menstrual periods may be irregular at first, but within a year or so, they should occur regularly every month. The first day of the bloody discharge marks the beginning of the monthly menstrual cycle. A 28-day cycle is average, but it can be as short as 20 days or as long as 35 days and still be normal.

The length of your period also can vary. Though it averages four or five days, some girls menstruate for only three days, others as long as seven or more.

Maybe you're asking the big question right now about sexual maturation: Am I normal? Let's look at some typical concerns that young teens have.

Debbie was the first in her crowd to enter puberty. She started maturing at the beginning of fifth grade and was self-conscious because none of her girlfriends were developing like her. Debbie slouched so she wouldn't seem so tall and, especially, she hunched her shoulders to disguise her gently rounding breasts.

But the other kids noticed she was different. Some of the guys rolled their eyes at her or made remarks as they passed her locker. Her best friend was envious and a little spiteful that Debbie attracted this attention. She suggested maybe Debbie wasn't quite "normal" in her development.

Debbie's mother assured her that each girl has a timetable, and that she should feel glad and proud that she was beginning to become a woman. At Debbie's pleading, her mother helped her pick out a brassiere, size Triple A, and they bought her new jeans and sweaters that weren't tight across the breast. Debbie decided growing up wasn't so bad after all.

Her friend, Kathleen, matured very late. By eighth grade, she was the only girl who didn't yet have a feminine figure. Most girls were menstruating, but Kathy hadn't yet experienced her first period. "I feel like a freak" she said unhappily; she felt sure that something was physically wrong. She confided to Debbie, "I'm never going to have a boyfriend. I'll never get married or have children."

Many girls worry about early or late maturation, but others compare themselves to their classmates and fret over being too tall, too skinny, not shapely enough, being overweight, having acne. Above all, most teens your age don't want to be different.

The important thing is to be comfortable with your own timetable and with your unique physical characteristics, which will be a little different from those of anyone you know. You will develop according to traits inherited from your family.

Furthermore, you'll mature sexually when your body is ready to do so, just as when you were born: not when your folks expected it, but when you were ready to make your grand entrance into the world!

Special hormones called estrogen and progesterone signal the changes, a little like an alarm clock going off. You may groan and complain when that alarm rings early in the morning. But in the case of hormones waking up your sexual nature, welcome the wakeup! Get ready to rise and shine in the bright light of adolescence!

Questions for Reflection/Discussion

1. Think of three words to describe how you feel about your body. Are these positive? If not, what do they express? What can you do to make them more positive?

2. Do you worry about menstruation? Do you have questions that no one has answered? How can you get an answer?

3. Would it bother you to be "different" from your friends? Why? Why not?

8~

Going Deeper

Let's look more carefully at the wonderful way the female body is made and how it functions. First, let's use some technically correct names for your sexual and reproductive system.

As you are probably aware, you have both external and internal genitalia, or genitals—another name for the sexual parts.

Between the legs, where the pubic hair grows, there's a double, padded mound called the vulva. Where these mounds of skin come together, they have the appropriate name, labia (Latin for "lips"), and they cover the opening to the vagina. The vagina is one of three body openings in this area. The others are the urinary opening and the anus, which is the bowel opening.

It is through the vaginal opening that the menstrual flow comes out. This also is the opening where the penis is inserted during sexual intercourse. The vagina is the passageway from the uterus to the outside of your body and serves as the corridor for the emerging baby, moving from the uterus to the outside world in birth.

If you feel a little embarrassed or uneasy thinking about all of this, that really is okay. We're talking about a very private part of the female body, one which is reserved for the deepest and most personal happenings in life. At the same time, I hope you feel a certain awe as you consider the marvel of God's creation of you as a woman. This creation is beautiful and good, something to be cherished and cared for with respect.

You may have heard about another sexual part called the hymen. This is a flexible fold of thin tissue over the vaginal opening and normally is intact in virgins. But, contrary to common belief, the hymen is not always in place and so its absence can't be used as a proof that a girl or woman has had sexual relations.

Deeper inside your body are other sexual organs. There is the cervix, a thick circular structure which is the lower part of the uterus. Then, there is the uterus itself, which we often refer to as the womb. If you're Catholic, you probably have said the Hail Mary many times, including the words: "Blessed is the fruit of thy womb." Now you can guess, if you haven't already, that the "fruit" of Mary's womb was Jesus. Jesus lived and grew in Mary's uterus, just as every child has lived in her own mother's womb while preparing to be born.

The uterus is an inverted pear-shaped organ about four inches long and it has the marvelous ability to stretch and greatly enlarge as the child grows bigger. Its lining, called the endometrium, is what is sloughed off in menstruation.

Two tubes, called fallopian tubes, are attached to the uterus on each side. The two ovaries, in which thousands of immature egg cells, called ova, are stored, are each located near the opening of one of the tubes. Once each month, about 14 days before menstruation is expected, one of the eggs ripens in one of the ovaries and travels from the ovary through the fallopian tube toward the uterus. This process is what we call ovulation.

Meanwhile, the uterus gets ready to receive the egg, which might grow into a baby. The uterus sponges up blood and other liquids to nourish the egg in case it is fertilized by the male sperm and implants itself on the wall of the uterus.

However, if the woman does not have sexual relations, the egg will not be fertilized and will live for only two or three days. Then it will disintegrate and be washed out of the uterus through the vagina, along with the bloody lining. This means that no baby was conceived by the joining of egg and sperm, and so the soft, nesting place prepared for the egg is not needed.

Questions for Reflection/Discussion

1. What is your biggest concern about growing up? How do you deal with this: talk to others, get information, etc.?

2. What was there in this section, if anything, that surprised you? Pleased you? Bothered you? Explain your response.

3. How would you describe being a sexual person?

~ 9

Menstruation: Badge of Womanhood

Some women and girls feel very negative about menstruation. They refer to it as "the curse" or describe themselves as being "sick" during their period. They dislike the whole business and, deep down, they are ashamed of being a woman, somehow feeling unclean and inferior because of the menstruation process.

There are cultural reasons for this attitude. According to a study by Tampax, a company that produces tampons, 35 percent of Americans think that menstruation affects a woman's ability to think and 30 percent believe you must limit your physical activities during your period.

Such misconceptions stem from the past when, in many parts of the world, menstruation and reproduction were not understood. The flow of blood was considered abnormal or a sign of evil spirits, and menstruating women actually were isolated from the rest of the tribe. And most men believed women were actually less intelligent and capable than they, especially during menstruation.

These faulty attitudes are from earlier times, but somehow many of them have been handed down from generation to generation. And so, even today some women continue to be uncomfortable and ashamed of their natural body functions.

I wholeheartedly encourage you not to fall into this mindset. Instead, recognize menstruation for what it really is: an essential aspect of your emerging womanliness and a sign that, physically, you now or soon will be able to bear a child. Of course, emotionally and socially, you won't be ready for motherhood for quite a long time, but menstruation is the important first step.

There's another "old wives' tale" which says that when you're having your period, you're sick. It's true that during menstruation many girls have some pain and discomfort: cramps, headache, or fatigue. You might feel depressed or sad for no reason you can think of or have wide mood swings. You may be tense and anxious just before you begin to menstruate. But be confident that it's your hormones talking and that menstruation is a good sign that your reproductive system is operating in healthy fashion. Such discomfort normally is *not* a sign of anything wrong.

The best thing you can do, beside feeling good about your womanly self, is to keep a normal, active routine. Even if you're in a little discomfort, continue to get out with your friends, to engage in all the projects and hobbies at home and school that interest you. It will help to keep you in good spirits.

Some girls we know keep track of their menstrual cycle by marking the first day of their period on a calendar. Your monthly cycle begins on the first day that you menstruate and finishes on the last day before you begin to menstruate again. This cycle will occur over and over again throughout your reproductive years.

If you know the length of your average cycle, you can figure approximately when your next period will arrive and this can help you schedule certain activities and be ready with adequate protection.

Many teens are very self-conscious during menstruation. Candy was anxious that a heavy flow would stain her clothing and create an embarrassing odor. Margie spent hours in front of the bathroom mirror, peering at blemishes that she claimed covered her face whenever she was menstruating. Noel thought that everyone at school knew when she was having her period by the tell-tale ridges that showed when she was wearing a sanitary pad.

Good personal habits, hygiene, and a positive and confident attitude will eliminate most such concerns.

You may have heard that you shouldn't get into water during your period. This, too, is a carryover from the past. Truth is, taking a shower or bath is perfectly okay; in fact, daily bathing is a must because you'll feel, look, and smell better! Just don't use very hot or cold water.

You probably will perspire more than usual, so don't forget deodorant and maybe some fragrant dusting powder. You will need to gently wash the external genitalia to prevent unpleasant odor.

It's perfectly permissible to wash your hair during your period. And having four daughters of my own, I know nothing will stop you from doing that anyway! Just avoid becoming chilled or getting in a draft. And, please, my young friend, don't run for the school bus with your hair dripping wet in 10–degree weather!

As for exercise and sports, that would have been a no–no once upon a time. But we know now that exercise in moderation is good for you and will help relieve pre-menstrual tension and occasional cramps. Even swimming is okay, but the caution on chilling applies here, too. You will need to use internal tampons rather than pads while swimming.

If you're into strenuous activity, pay attention to your body and the messages it sends you. Our bodies and minds really do work together in a wonderful way, and the body will communicate discomfort or pain if you're overdoing it. You need to heed its signals.

At first, your menstrual periods may be irregular and this

is not a sign of a problem. You may skip a month once in a while. Such irregularity usually happens as your organs adjust to your new body cycle. Also, irregular cycles occasionally are caused by strong emotions or stress, changes in routine and overly strenuous physical activity. You might want to see your doctor if your period continues to be irregular or if you frequently skip months.

As for the menstrual flow itself, some girls fear that they are losing large amounts of blood. You might be surprised to know that an average flow of blood during the four or five days of menstruation only totals about four ounces—half a cup or so—nothing to be worried about.

You can use either a tampon or sanitary pad while you are menstruating. Most sanitary pads available today have adhesive strips that attach easily to your underwear. Change pads often, though, because when exposed to air, the blood will develop an unpleasant odor.

Tampons are worn internally and they do a good job when you aren't flowing heavily. They are inserted through a slit in the hymen, so they don't break the membrane. However, "toxic shock syndrome," a serious and sometimes life-threatening disorder, has been reported in a small number of menstruating girls and women who were using tampons. Although rare, it can be fatal and may be somewhat more common among teenage girls than among older women. Symptoms of TSS include a sudden high fever, diarrhea, fainting, and vomiting. Tell your mother and see a doctor if you use tampons and some of these symptoms occur.

If you do use tampons, you can decrease the risk of TSS by changing your tampon frequently, at least every three to four hours, more often if your flow is heavy. You can get more information about TSS from the school nurse or at the library. Talk to your Mom about it and carefully weigh the pros and cons of using tampons.

Above all, don't be ashamed or apologetic because you are menstruating. Stay calm and be matter of fact if others become aware of it or if they joke or show in other ways how uncomfortable they are. Remind them that this is the normal and fantastic sign of becoming a woman.

You may have heard of "change of life," more properly called menopause. It occurs when a woman's ovaries decrease their production of estrogen and she stops menstruating. At this season of her life, she no longer is able to have a child.

But going through menopause should not signal the end of a woman's active sexual life. And certainly, she doesn't become less a woman, although sometimes mature women feel they have lost their sexual attractiveness when they know they no longer can bear children. Normally, women go into menopause some time between their mid–forties and early fifties.

Questions for Reflection/Discussion

1. Who told you about menstruation? Under what circumstances? Did you feel good learning about these facts? Why? Why not?

2. How do you feel, physically and emotionally, during your period? Are you proud or embarrassed? Why is this?

3. If a younger girl asked you about "the curse," what would you say to her?

10~

Boys: The Awe-ful Wonderful Difference

I hope you noticed the misspelled word "awe-ful" in this title. It's a play on words and here's what I mean: Girls and boys in grade school often don't have much use for one another. They ignore one another, stick with their own sex, and, in general, think members of the opposite sex are boring and an awful pain. Boys tease girls and girls do their best to ignore them.

Then, junior high arrives, and—girls first—each starts to notice that the other sex may not be so bad after all. Pretty soon, girls find boys the most fascinating creatures around. They're in awe of those obvious differences: how strong he is, how tough he looks, how he smiles, the funny things he says. Usually, boys don't catch on to the "awe-ful" wonderful difference as quickly as girls. But before long, both realize it was a great idea God had in creating two sexes.

Your mother and father and your grandparents probably went through the same cycle of disinterest, then attraction.

But in earlier days, sexual and biological information usually wasn't taught in school or freely discussed at home. If you're from a family where sex is an open topic, you will be wise to take advantage of the chance to ask questions and hear from adults who've had a lifetime of experience in being sexual persons.

Your mother may well have given you an understanding about your own growth and maturation. She may have prepared you for the onset of menstruation. But, most likely, neither she nor your father has offered information about male development.

That's the purpose of this chapter. It's good for you to learn about male sexuality because it will help you to understand boys and to have respect for the marvelous bodies that God gave them.

On the average, boys enter puberty two or three years later than girls, between the ages of 13 and 15. Like you, they experience a spurt in physical size and often feel clumsy and awkward when—suddenly—their feet are big, their arms get all tangled up, and their emotions, like yours, are a constant surprise.

While girls develop in the breasts and hips, guys broaden in the shoulders and begin to develop hard muscles. Their voices deepen and sometimes, to their great embarrassment, crack in mid-sentence. They also grow hair on their bodies. Especially, they grow hair on the face which makes shaving a "must," even though no one but they can see the downy fuzz that covers their cheeks and upper lip.

All these changes are brought on by the production of hormones, coordinated by that "master gland," the pituitary. A chemical impulse goes from the pituitary gland to the sex glands which haven't functioned until now. This message signals the beginning of rapid and uneven sexual development, starting with physical growth and culminating in the production of the male sperm.

Unlike a girl's, most of a boy's sexual organs are outside his body. There are the testicles, or testes, which are the sex glands that produce androgens, which bring about physical changes. The testes are two ball-shaped organs, which are often referred to as "balls" or "nuts." These are contained in a soft, thick-skinned sac called the scrotum. The scrotum keeps the testicles in place and protects them from injury, especially in rough, contact sports.

You might wonder: why are the testicles dangling around down there in such an unlikely place? Why aren't they safely tucked inside the body, as your sexual parts are? Here's where you can appreciate more of God's intricate design.

The testicles are the organs that produce sperm and, as you know, sperm cells fertilize the female egg cell. But in order for sperm to survive, they must be kept at a certain temperature. The internal temperature of the body is too high. So the scrotum acts as a regulator. At times, it stretches downward and moves the testicles away from the body where there's too much heat. But when it's real cold outside, the scrotum wrinkles upward to get near the body's warmth. Amazing!

The penis is the other important external sex organ in the male. This tube-like part hangs down over the scrotum and is the organ through which semen or urine flow to the outside of the body. But these two processes never occur at the same time.

When a baby boy is born, his penis is covered with a soft layer of skin, called the foreskin. When the male is only a few days old, many people for religious or hygenic reasons have this skin removed. This surgical procedure is called circumcision. Do you remember that Jesus was circumcised as part of a Jewish religious rite?

Internally, adult males have a gland called the prostate which produces fluid that mixes with sperm cells to form semen. Before mixing with this fluid, sperm are stored in something called the seminal vesicle.

Finally, in something of a parallel with the female's fallopian tubes, males have seminal ducts and these narrow tubes carry sperm from the testes to the urethra, the tube in the penis that leads to the outside.

As a young man continues to develop, more and more sperm cells are produced and every once in a while, nature will decide there are too many and will push them out of the body. The way it happens is that the penis becomes erect, that is, it temporarily builds up, swelling or enlarging until it is much bigger and longer than normal. When it becomes erect, a muscle is tripped in the back of the penis, sending out the milky fluid. This is called an ejaculation.

But young boys may call it a "wet dream" because it often occurs at night and may be accompanied by a stimulating dream.

A boy also may ejaculate when the penis is stimulated by physical activity, too tight clothing, or a sexual urge brought on by the sight of a sexy woman or through intimate kissing or touching of a girl. When the stimulus gets too strong and erection takes place, ejaculation may happen even if the boy tries to signal it to stop.

Because of how they are made, most boys are sexually aroused much more quickly than girls. This is why some people believe that as a girl you are more responsible for moral behavior than the boys you are with. I don't fully believe this, but we'll return to the question later.

The most important thing to know is that the male body, like the girl's, is beautifully, wonderfully made. As a boy matures, this is a sign—as it is for you—that he is growing into adulthood and that some day he too can become a parent.

Unfortunately, this idea isn't very popular in our culture, which bombards boys with a message that girls and sex are there to be physically enjoyed and experienced without restraint. Society pounds this theme home repeatedly, and it's a challenge for boys, with the strong urges and quick sexual response they have, to keep a Christian sense of awe and respect for the holiness of human sexuality.

Questions for Reflection/Discussion

1. Are boys your main priority at this point in your life? What and who ranks ahead of them? Why?

2. How easy is it to talk to your parents about boys? Can you comfortably ask questions about male development?

3. What fact(s) about male sexuality surprises you? How does this information make you feel? Why?

4. Do you believe that boys have equal responsibility to be chaste? If so, why? If not, why don't they?

~ 11
The Challenge of Adolescence

So far, we've focused on physical growth and maturation. But the most exciting thing for all young people your age is to realize and work toward what's on the other side of adolescence: adulthood!

An adolescent is a person on the move. And—no question about it—it's a time of confusion and change. In a way, you're half-child, half-adult, and some mornings when you get up, it's hard to figure out which half you are that day.

You may long for the safe feeling of being a little kid again, yet you also anticipate enjoying the privileges of adult life. On some days, you feel uncertain, scared, even angry; on others, high, enthusiastic, and supremely confident. You have new feelings and dreams that make you want to be alone at times. But being with your group of friends matters a lot. You're on an unpredictable, emotional roller-coaster!

A helpful way to think of adolescence is to see it as a time of tasks you need to complete so you can move on to adulthood. Here are four basic and very important tasks of adolescence.

1. Declaring Your Values Who am I? What do I believe in? What is important to me? These are the questions you begin to ask as you reach teen years. All through childhood, you've accepted and believed quite naturally all your parents said and did. But most teens now begin to question and search out other points of view on every kind of issue: clothes, movies, manners, politics, religion, sex, marriage, and baseball teams.

It's not that your family's values aren't good. It's that you need to look at them with fresh, objective eyes, to compare them to what your friends say, what you hear in school, what's on television, and to what your own voice inside you says. In some matters, you may reject what your family believes. This causes your parents to be upset and often creates conflict between you and them. But it's a pretty normal part of growing up.

When you have more experience—and less need to strike out on your own—we hope you may return to your family's values and embrace them as your own. Or you may integrate these with some newfound values to create new beliefs that are truly yours.

For now, though, it can be a confusing time where you feel like you're throwing everything out, but you don't know what you're putting in their place. I would encourage you, as part of this task, to go slow in rejecting all you've absorbed in childhood. Most of these values are sound and valuable and will stand the test of time if you give them a chance. This establishment of a value system is closely connected to your second task.

2. Separating from Parents Somewhere during adolescence all young people need to loosen the tight bonds they have with their parents. The closer you feel to Mom or Dad or both, the more painful it's going to be for both of you.

They think you're rejecting them and they're hurt and surprised. After all, they've loved you and cared for you all your life! And you feel guilty and wish things could be warm and close again. But somehow you can't live with that tight bond any more, except on the lonely days.

You know, deep inside, that you still love and need your parents very much. And you really want them to be proud of you. But you also know that you've got to push forward if you're going to become your own woman. Somewhere in the next few years, you need to say, I am a person; I am *me!*

During this period, your family may worry a lot about where you're headed. "How did we go wrong? What does she see in those crazy friends of hers?" Dad asks Mom. "How could she fight us all the time and reject everything we've tried to teach her?" worries Mom.

It helps a lot to let them know that you still love them, that you don't want to hurt them, that they've done a good job of raising you. But you also need to remind them that you're growing up, and that searching out new ways is part of the process. Ask them to help you by letting go a little.

Above all, this is not the time to get involved in dangerous or damaging behavior—just to prove you're grown up.

Ann's parents were very strict, and when she reached her sophomore year in high school, Ann still wasn't allowed to single date nor to stay out past 11 on weekends. In defiance, Ann began to sneak off with boys from her crowd and, because she had so little experience, got deeply involved with a senior. She became sexually active and within months Ann was pregnant. A basically innocent and responsible girl had to face the trauma of bearing a child when she was still a child herself.

Roseann lived with her divorced mother and younger brother and saw her father every other weekend. Her Dad allowed her a good bit of freedom, encouraging her to have a drink with him when they went to dinner. For her sixteenth birthday, he bought her a car. Roseann loved to pick up all her friends after school and joyride around town. Sometimes they got beer from one of their houses and drank it behind the school football field.

It bugged Roseann that her mother objected to the car.

She knew Mom would have a fit about the drinking, but after all, Roseann thought, wasn't she entitled to some freedom? When was her Mom going to recognize she wasn't a child any more?

We can only hope that Roseann and her friends don't become traffic statistics or alcoholics, all in the name of independence!

Through this challenging time, two-way communication between your parents and you is the key. And even as you express your growing independence, you also need to listen carefully and respectfully and to continue to learn from these experienced people who love you so much.

3. Finding Sexual Identity This may be the scariest task of any because it's hard to act on Christian values in a world that makes sex so cheap. The stakes are high. You can do terrible damage to yourself, your future, and your parents' confidence in you by impulsive choices which are influenced by others who see sex only as a plaything.

Establishing sexual identity is complicated. It involves understanding and accepting the physical changes of puberty, knowing and cherishing your body as a beautiful part of God's gift to you. It means enjoying that you are a woman and understanding what this means, and doesn't mean, in our world.

Defining your sexuality includes recognizing the culture's notion of female attractiveness, but rejecting false standards of physical perfection. You know: being a "10" with large breasts, a tiny waist, a sexy body with no bulges. Unfortunately, many people leave out the more lasting definition of a beautiful woman: someone who is caring, honest, loving, and honorable. Your personality and character, as well as your body, are what make you beautiful.

Establishing a sexual identity also includes discovering that you have both feminine and masculine traits within your personality. This means that, by nature, you may be emotional and affectionate ("feminine"), but also strong-willed and assertive ("masculine").

I've purposely used labels here that are our society's typical way of describing men and women. Really, these labels are stereotypes and for too long we've accepted very narrow definitions of what men and women ought to be like. We based these on characteristics that we thought described typical men and women.

For women, this included being "weak," "gentle," "passive," "timid," "emotional," "unpredictable," "loving," "agreeable," and so on. Men were described as "strong," "intellectual," "athletic," "aggressive," "brave," "powerful," "mechanical," and so on.

Just think of the way we've stereotyped the sexes: "Big boys don't cry"..."the weaker sex"..."crazy woman driver"..."strong silent male"..."woman is the heart of the home"...and that classic verse:

Sugar and spice and everything nice,
That's what little girls are made of.
Snakes and snails and puppy-dog tails,
That's what little boys are made of.

The truth is that often there are some typical personality differences among men and women. But most of these aren't inborn. They are shaped by the child's upbringing as a girl or a boy and by the roles each sex is supposed to play in the society we live in.

Today, we understand more clearly than in earlier times that being fully human involves having a wide range of personal characteristics, and that these aren't restricted to one sex. So, instead of conforming to someone else's idea of femininity, your task is to know, accept, and *be* who you really are.

To establish your sexual identity involves finding your "sexual style," your way of relating socially to boys. It means becoming able to form real friendships with them and developing some skills in dating and girl–boy communication. You need to discover what you like and don't like in different boys. And you must learn to deal appropriately with sexual feelings, both yours and those of the boys you date.

Establishing your sexual identity is a long process that will occupy you all through adolescence and into adult life.

4. Making Vocational Choices Each of us as Christians has one fundamental vocation: to believe in Jesus and his teachings and to try to live our lives as lovingly and faithfully as he lived his.

Before long, you will be making long-range plans for your future: college or a job? Marriage out of high school...after college...or no plans to marry at all? A choice of careers—social service, medicine, journalism, business, nursing, teaching. You may choose to spend your life working with the poor here or in another country. Or you might discover you want to live a vowed religious life by becoming a nun.

"Being a wife and mother" is the lifelong hope of many young women, and they don't go beyond that dream. This is a wonderful and valuable way to find happiness as well as build a better world. I believe that raising four wonderful and responsible daughters has been my most important and fulfilling accomplishment.

But you also need to look at the many options there are for your whole lifetime. You are called by God to develop all of your talents and gifts. This requires that you prepare yourself early in life with a good education, and that you explore the work and career possibilities that best suit you.

Your decisions about vocation may seem a long way off, but the day-to-day choices you make now—to study hard, to learn from your parents, to live as a person of faith and conscience, to respect your sexuality—will help you move toward responsible vocational decisions in your future. Each calling in life can be holy when you love God and other people and you serve them in a kind and generous way.

As a teenager faced with the four important tasks of adolescence, is it any wonder you sometimes feel overwhelmed? Maybe you didn't realize this is what's going on in your life. So it helps to name it and to see that the tasks you're working on are necessary and very valuable. Be patient and remember: God's not finished with you yet!

Questions for Reflection/Discussion

1. In the last two years, in what ways have you changed? What is the single most important way? Explain.

2. What are your most important values? Where did these come from?

3. Do you think that society supports Christian beliefs and values about sex? What are the differences, if any?

4. How do you feel about your parents these days? How do they feel about you? Do you listen to each other? Do you need to communicate better? How can you?

5. Make a list of all the "feminine" and "masculine" traits you see in yourself. What does this say about sexual stereotypes?

6. What are your most important long-range dreams for the future? Do you think these will change? How?

12~

The Dating Scene

Dating may be the most important thing in your young life. Or maybe you aren't interested yet. Instead, you may at this time want to concentrate on studies or devote yourself to becoming a great swimmer or basketball player or musician. Or you work after school to help support the family. Some girls don't date because they're shy or afraid or just not ready.

You should know that any and all of these attitudes are normal and okay. Just as in physical development, everyone has her own timetable for social maturation. Be comfortable with yours and don't be hurried by your friends or another person's expectations.

Some girls worry because no one asks them out. But many boys in first or second year of high school aren't yet interested in dating girls. Or they're shy and afraid of being turned down. Remember, on the average boys mature about two years later than you do, and they need to be allowed to grow up at their own rate.

In recent years, there has been a good change among teenagers compared with earlier generations. Today's young people seem to prefer to run around in crowds rather than single date, and this really is a more ideal way to get to know one another. It makes closeness to the opposite sex a lot less scary for both guys and girls. You can kid around and be yourself and meet up with all sorts of people without anyone misunderstanding. You can even experiment with being different persons and discover the you that pleases you most. Best of all, you can develop friendships without it having to be a big deal.

A non-romantic friendship is a way to get to know the opposite sex, to understand what makes boys tick, to get a male reaction to problems you're having! Such friendship is a precious thing.

With all the different groups that hang around, eventually you'll find one where you fit in. Sooner or later, you'll begin to go out. It will all happen in good time. Don't be over-eager. Remember, many slow starters end up as very popular girls because they build confidence and skills in their early teen years.

Some young girls, determined to get a boyfriend, approach dating in a less-than-helpful fashion. Consider these three girls:

Cassandra, 14, thinks the greatest way to attract guys is with flashy good looks. She wears sexy and overly sophisticated clothes, mauve eye shadow, and an exotic moussed hair style. She and her friend, Marcie, hang around a mall where the older crowd gathers. Already, they are getting involved with two high school juniors although they're forbidden by their mothers to date.

Marcie's sister, Janice, 17, is afraid her boyfriend will leave her unless she has sex with him so she's given in to his demands. She feels guilty about it, and having sex isn't all she thought it would be, but she "loves" Pete, so what can she do?

Cassandra, Marcie, and Janice have unfortunate ideas

about what will make them popular. They think sex is the only way to get a guy's attention. It may be the quickest way, because, as you've probably noticed, teenage boys are turned on by sexy actions and appearance.

But, what are these girls giving away? And how long does such "popularity" last? If I may recall ancient times (when I was young), I remember girls who flouted their sexuality, and the guys loved it! They had dates whenever they wanted. But by junior year, the other girls were the ones the boys chased. Apparently, they found out there's more to enjoy about a girl than the physical side. And the girls who used sex to attract boys not only had lost the desirable boyfriends but also their self-respect and their good name.

The most serious drawback of early dating is that it often leads to steady dating. Why do teens go steady? Young people your age have told me these reasons:

1. They want to experience "love," to have an intimate, secure relationship.
2. It's a way to prove they're grown up, no longer "just a kid."
3. "Everyone does it"; it's the accepted thing in their crowd.
4. Some want to be sure of having a date for parties and school affairs.

As good as these reasons may seem, the reasons not to go steady are better. Having a "steady" really limits the variety of boys you meet; you miss not only a lot of fun but the different kinds of experience that help you know the sort of person you might someday want to choose for your own.

Going steady may lead to very deep emotional ties that interfere with all the other aspects of your teen life. You become preoccupied with romance and your school work suffers. You lose interest in extracurricular activities, your circle of girlfriends, spending time with the family. You no longer have enthusiasm for all the things that once mattered.

You quit the volleyball team because it takes too much time away from your boyfriend. You don't have free time for your volunteer work at the nursing home. Music lessons fall by the wayside. Nothing else counts except being with your boyfriend. That may seem wonderful, but this is the time in your life when reaching out for all kinds of experience and opportunity can help you to grow into an accomplished and interesting young person.

Sometimes the price paid for going steady is even more serious. Increased physical intimacy, loss of self-respect, perhaps pregnancy or venereal disease is the result. And all too often, a boy grows tired of the girl with whom he has had sex, and he leaves in search of a new girl to "conquer."

Consider that the average girl in the United States doesn't marry until her early to mid-twenties. This means you have a long time ahead of you for dating and finding that special someone. Take it easy; don't rush the process; there's lots of time!

How can you improve your chances for a happy and successful social life? Some people would say there are three basic ways, all of them important: 1) by being physically attractive; 2) by having a good personality; 3) by being a person of character.

1. Physical Attractiveness Obviously, appearance matters. Good grooming—shiny hair, clean, fresh skin, a gleaming and healthy smile, a pleasant fragrance—all make you a nice person to be around.

Your clothes don't have to be elaborate or expensive or trendy. If they're appropriately combined, becoming to your body shape and clean and pressed, they will add to your attractive appearance and give you confidence.

Getting seven or eight hours of sleep a night, regular physical exercise, eating a balanced diet of healthy food and keeping a happy and optimistic attitude will insure good health, which is the foundation of beauty.

Without overemphasizing physical beauty, you need to realize that a well-proportioned body is an asset. If you're overweight, don't crash diet, but ask your doctor or health teacher for a plan, and stick with it! A balanced diet will pay off in good looks and a strong sense of being in charge of your life.

Obviously, a diet of junk food, smoking, drugs, and alcohol will hurt you physically and slowly eat away at the emotional and spiritual beauty that is yours. Being at peace with God, yourself, and others puts a sparkle in your eye and a smile in your voice. It draws people to you and is what some people call "beauty from within."

2. Personality A good personality is the backbone of popularity. What traits attract teenagers? Ask yourself, what traits attract you? They're probably the same as what other young people are looking for.

According to various surveys, what matters to teens are such things as friendliness, a sense of humor, enthusiasm, someone who's fun, someone who's interested in what others have to say, and an easy-going way that reassures the other person.

Boys especially like girls who don't make fun or laugh at them, and who are good sports enough to be cheerful when plans don't turn out as expected.

The good thing to remember is that you can improve your personality to become more pleasing. For instance, anybody can be friendly in a sincere way. You can say hello, smile, praise another person when they do something nice, be welcoming to a new kid at school.

Enthusiasm is a wonderful trait that can be developed. Becoming enthused and challenged by each day's events, really getting into the spirit of things makes those around you also excited and enthusiastic. Don't you enjoy a person who has a zest for life? *You* can be that kind of person!

Carrying on a conversation, especially with the opposite sex, scares most young teens. They think they have to be great talkers or the life of the party. Instead, when you're with someone you don't know very well, you can simply think of what is going on at school, in world headlines, on the sports field or among your friends, and make a comment about it. Then ask the other person what he or she thinks. You respond to their views—and presto! you're conversing.

It's really important to say what you think, to have your own, perhaps different, point of view. Be honest, and above all *be yourself*. Don't put on airs or pretend to agree just to go along with the crowd. Be warm and friendly, but don't think you have to laugh all the time in order to be a fun person.

And there's another way, besides talking, to be a great conversationalist. Someone once said, "God gave us two ears and only one mouth, so we should listen twice as much as we talk!" If you're feeling shy, try being a good listener. This means you genuinely listen in an active way to what others are sharing; you respond with encouragement, nods and smiles and genuine interest in their ideas and feelings. There is no one who doesn't enjoy a person who cares about what the other thinks.

Being a good listener has other benefits: it takes your mind off yourself and you become less self-conscious. You really find out what the person is all about, and maybe you discover how much everyone has the same needs and concerns.

Finally, listening rather than talking all the time gives you a reputation as a really neat person to be with, someone who can be counted on to be concerned about others.

3. Character That's the third dimension of who you are. It's related to personality, but it's on a deeper level. Character has to do with your values, your beliefs about yourself, your feelings about people. Personality might be the topping on the cake, but character is the dough, the substance that makes you an attractive and lovable person.

People of character are truthful and sincere with others. They're kind to other persons, even the nerd who keeps asking them out or the brother who bugs them. They don't cheat so they can make a higher grade or a better impression.

They try to be helpful at home and with others who need their assistance. They can be depended on. When they say they will do something, they follow through.

People of character know that God is important in their life and they're not ashamed to pray and encourage others to do the same. They think enough of themselves to resist the pressure to go along with the crowd. They know who they are, and they like (and love) themselves. They speak up on issues they believe in, even if these are unpopular with others.

A person of character is humble enough to admit when she is wrong. If she hurts someone's feelings, she is willing to say she's sorry. Character is built slowly over many years; it isn't one great act of courage, but is many small deeds done with consistency and good motives.

Gerri was a friendly but insecure freshman who thought having a boyfriend was the way to prove, mostly to herself, that she was lovable. So when a guy asked her out, Gerri became the pursuer. If he didn't call her, she called him. She made sure he knew where she'd be after every class. She gave him expensive gifts and hinted about going steady. She pouted if he didn't sit with her at the games.

Most boys were scared off by Gerri, even though they liked her and were flattered by her attention. Eventually, they stopped asking her out and she never understood why.

Joe was a big-time braggart. He tried so hard to impress a girl that he bored her with exaggerated stories of all the great things he had accomplished. And he showed off in restaurants, at shopping malls, and other public places—all because Joe wanted desperately to be liked and admired. Instead, the girls were embarrassed and laughed at him behind his back.

Then there was Barbara, who all through high school couldn't seem to find a boyfriend or a crowd where she fit in, even though she was smart and cute. The problem was that Barbara was a pain to be with. She made sarcastic remarks, talked behind people's backs, and put them down while trying to build herself up. If the kids wanted to go out for pizza or planned a movie, Barbara always complained; it was never what she wanted to do. She had few lasting friends. Unfortunately, no one was brave enough to tell her the reason was her negative personality.

Natalie was determined to belong. She went along with everybody, agreed with the majority opinion on every issue and, what got on everyone's nerves, she laughed constantly. Natalie's big problem was she was afraid to be herself, afraid to share her feelings and ideas honestly.

No one ever found out she was a fantastic ping-pong player or that she had lived in India when she was little. Or that she kept a diary and wrote poetry and cried at old television movies. Her friends never knew the *real* Natalie and she realized that she wasn't accepted for herself. The reason? She had never really shown herself. Most often, she felt lonely and hypocritical because she knew the image she put out wasn't really her.

The message from all these examples is pretty simple: it's not so important to find the right person or crowd; it is important to *be* the right person, someone who's nice to be around, is interesting and enthusiastic, and isn't so insecure that she either can't be herself or must constantly be in the spotlight.

Be willing to express honest appreciation for what you discover in other people. But, perhaps, gentle criticism is a greater gift when someone is hurting herself with unattractive or destructive behavior. If you know someone like Natalie, you might encourage her to risk showing her true self. You could privately tip Joe off that he doesn't need to be a world-beater to be liked, that his stories just turn people off. Gerri and Barbara need to hear, from someone who cares, what effect their behavior is having on their relationships with other kids. If someone is hurt or discouraged, your word of support can encourage and comfort. When someone has failed, he or she needs to know that failing in some effort doesn't make anyone a failure as a person.

It takes a lot of conscious effort and discipline to develop the physical attractiveness, personality, and character that will make you a well-liked and respected person. But it pays off not only in friendship, but in the joy of discovering that you are becoming the best possible person you can be, the person God had in mind when God created you!

Questions for Reflection/Discussion

1. What do you look for in a boy? In a girl? Are the expectations similar? How are they different? Why are they different?

2. What do you expect in a boy's behavior on a date? How do you let him know your expectations?

3. What are your strengths as a potential date? What do you need to work on?

4. What was your "most embarrassing moment" with a boy? What did you learn from it? Can you laugh about it today?

5. Is Saturday night a "waste" without a date? What do you do when this happens? How do you spend your evening?

~ 13

How Will I Know When I'm in Love?

Love! It's probably the most versatile and overused word in the English language! It means many, many things to each of us, and different things to different people:

You love your pre-washed jeans, I love my word processor. You love kittens, I love trees, your Dad loves his Toyota, your best friend loves Don Johnson, people love their country, your boyfriend loves the Boston Celtics, you love your grandmother, your crowd loves nachos, all of us love being free. Get the idea?

The word "love" is used freely and sometimes mistakenly. We say "love" when we mean "like," "love" when we'd be more accurate saying "enjoy" or "appreciate." Also, there are different kinds of real love: the love of family or the love of friends, both of which can be very deep and strong and genuine.

But let's consider the word "love" in connection with man–woman relationships. You've been seeing a certain boy in class for two semesters. He shows up at the same parties as you. And suddenly you discover your heart pounds when he walks by. He has the warmest smile and he seems to want to talk to you. Twice you danced together and it was heaven! Could this be love?

With your heart and emotions engaged, you better define the word carefully. Because you may think it's love, really love, and you pour your heart and soul into the relationship—which is not at all what the boy has in mind—you may end up carrying a large flaming torch. You may think that you've lost your One True Love.

There's an old love song that goes: "Falling in love with Love is falling for make-believe; falling in love with Love is playing the fool...." The song is trying to say that all of us, and maybe adolescents especially, fall into this state because we like the *feelings* attached to being "in love": the breathless excitement, the warm and romantic emotion, the thrilling thought that this gorgeous person thinks I'm beautiful and dreams of me at night. Who could resist such pleasure? Who wants to? Let's just not confuse it with the real thing.

Old-timers in the love game have found out that emotions that put on the face of love can be a clever imposter named infatuation. And the person who's head-over-heels in "love" won't pull off the mask because it feels so good!

Don't get me wrong; infatuation is a delightful, normal, and okay thing, especially for teens. It's exciting and fun! One day you think you're going to die (he hasn't called), the next, you're riding the crest of the wave (he's coming over to see you). Infatuation is an emotional blast. *But it isn't love.*

Instead, it's a perfectly normal stage that people experience when they're maturing. At an early stage of adolescence, you might develop a crush on a rock star, a teacher, an athlete, or even someone your own sex, such as a friendly older student or the gym teacher. You idealize this person and fantasize about being with him; you extravagantly admire her as the ideal, lovable, and perfect person.

This is a good process. Actually, you're focusing on an idealized someone who is "safe" because they're not within your reach. You're practicing for the future when your "love" interest will be much more human and real. Being infatuated with a woman or girl gives you a model, someone you'd like to be like, someone who has characteristics that are very attractive.

Later, you move to boys your own age and here, too, the feelings can be very intense. Having crushes early in adolescence is perfectly okay. It prepares you for later relationships.

Infatuation is only a problem if you take it too seriously, making a pest of yourself with some celebrity or announcing your "love" to a teacher and getting a shocked and negative response! Infatuation also can be a problem if you mistake the normal strong feelings of a teen romance for genuine love, if you put too much trust in the permanence of these feelings that you and your boyfriend share. It's even more serious if you make major life decisions (having sex, getting married) based on a belief that the two of you are meant for each other for all time. Later, the breakup comes, and one or both of you suffer a broken heart. Make no mistake, just because it's infatuation doesn't mean it doesn't hurt!

How can you tell if it's love or infatuation? Here are some signs and comparisons:

1. Infatuation is instant....Love is slow. This means your romantic feelings develop quickly. It's "love at first sight" even before you know much about the other person. Love develops slowly, sometimes growing from a casual, even unfriendly relationship. Infatuation can't wait; it forces the issue. Love is patient and steady and allows friendship to ripen.

2. Infatuation is sexually focused....Love is person-centered. In infatuation, you can't keep your hands off each other. You just want to be alone and making out. Your good-nights get longer and longer and every kiss, every touch calls for more. Sexual attraction also may be strong in love, but there's so much more going on. It's the whole person that delights you, their sweet words, their strength and seriousness, the little jokes they play, the faith they have. You love it all, even without sex.

3. Infatuation triggers insecurity....Love brings confidence. One moment you're up, the next day you're down because of something he said or something foolish you did; that's infatuation. It can be painful; you're never really certain how he feels, or that he'll stay that way. In love, you know that nothing you've done that's petty or foolish will end the bond between you. Your feelings grow deeper and stronger day by day. It's a steady growth and you grow self-assured and confident because of it.

4. Infatuation wants just us....Love welcomes others. When a guy and girl are deeply infatuated, they concentrate on being alone. Their "love" is too precious to share with others; they become exclusive and stop wanting to be with their families or their crowd. They want privacy. When you're in love, this lovely spirit spills over into all your relationships: your friends, family, even strangers. You want to share your joy with others. Love makes you more than you've been before.

5. Infatuation emphasizes self....Love focuses on the other. If all you can think of is how good he makes you feel, how great it is to be seen with him, how gorgeous he thinks you are, you're infatuated. Infatuation puts the focus on you, gives you satisfaction, and if you're emotionally insecure, you run a greater risk of seeing infatuation as love. In love, you spend your time thinking of how to make him happy, how to be a better person to please him. Your self-preoccupation gives way to concentration on the beloved. And he has the same wish: to bring happiness and pleasure to you.

As I said earlier, infatuation isn't wrong; it's just a phase in your growth toward the mature capacity you'll have later for deep, true love, which is also sexual.

David Lorentz, who teaches human sexuality courses in a Catholic high school, writes:

> The students and I talk a lot about what isn't love, things like infatuation, need-fulfillment, fantasy....I might ask a guy what it means to make love. He thinks he's in love with that person, you know. Many times, there has been no thought about what she wants or needs.
>
> How can you say you love someone, that you can make love with someone, when you don't even know them? Knowing your own needs is a start, but it's still self-knowledge. Loves need to know each other!
>
> It isn't love when it's easier to touch than to talk, when kisses are easier than communication, when you're sexual partners but not necessarily friends.
>
> It isn't love when you want sex but refuse to take responsibility for what might happen: pregnancy, herpes, venereal disease.
>
> It isn't love when you use the feelings and body of another person to make yourself look like a winner, and then treat that person as a trophy, a thing that you won.
>
> It isn't love when you manipulate another person's emotions. "Prove your love by having sex with me."
>
> It isn't love when you put down your partner by making fun or betraying secrets, actions which violate his or her privacy and self-worth.
>
> Infatuation can lead to love, but it may not. The real starting point of any lasting love is friendship, that which you nudge and nurture and which blossoms one day into the intimacy of tender caring and commitment. When sexual love (not necessarily sexual acts) joins such friendship, we can with confidence call it Love.

These are wise words, to be pondered and referred to often in the next few years. Don't be afraid to feel the feelings that come to you as your friendship with a boy deepens into romance. But go slow and grow cautious about naming it Love.

Questions for Reflection/Discussion

1. Who are the people you "love"? Describe the different ways you love each one.

2. Have you ever been "in love"? How did you know it wasn't infatuation? What's the best way to tell if it's really love?

3. What are some good consequences of infatuation? What are the risks?

4. What are four things that real love can do for you?

~ 14
Time for More Questions

Q: Boys are so weird! One day they like you and treat you nice. The next day they act mean or stuck up. How can you figure out what's going on?

A: If a boy goes out of his way to be obnoxious, it could be because a girl has been chasing him and he's embarrassed by it. Or it very well might be because he likes her but doesn't know how to show it. Boys your age don't have much experience in how to treat girls they like, and they feel shy and awkward. Stay cool, offer a friendly smile, and give the boys a chance to grow up socially. If you help them get over their self-consciousness, they'll like you even more.

Q: I'm 13 and my mother won't let me wear makeup. How can I show her she's wrong?

A: Maybe "wrong" isn't the right word; try "cautious." She may be struggling to accept the fact that her daughter is growing up. Parents often can't realize their little girl is becoming a woman. Or she may be afraid you'll overdo it as some teens do, loading on the eye makeup, burying their young skin under heavy cosmetics. You need to strike a compromise with her, maybe a little blush, some lipstick, a touch of mascara if your lashes are pale. Your mother might be willing to go along with these moderate choices. If you're in high school, it's surely not too soon to start. If you're still in junior high, you might need to honor her wishes. Patience!

Q: I just found out about sex, I mean the act. I can't believe a man's penis can fit into the opening a woman has. Doesn't it hurt her?

A: First of all, the woman's vagina is very stretchy and it can accommodate any size penis. Second, when a married couple has sexual intercourse, there are many affectionate kisses, touches, and hugs which lead up to the act itself. This is because intercourse is supposed to be the loving and total giving of one person to the other. It's not intended as a quick and easy way to have pleasure. During what's called foreplay, as a couple expresses their love, the couple becomes sexually aroused and both the penis and the vagina become lubricated to prepare for the penis to enter comfortably. Under these conditions, intercourse is not painful.

Q: What is the clitoris?

A: It's a very sensitive organ, shaped somewhat like a very small penis, located outside the woman's vagina. It is a source of sexual stimulation and pleasure.

Q: I've only had one period and that was three months ago. Shouldn't I be having them every month now? I'm 14.

A: Not necessarily. The menstrual cycle often is quite irregular as a girl becomes mature, and many girls don't menstruate until your age. You should become more regular in the months ahead. If not, you might want to see a doctor to be sure there's nothing holding up your development.

Q: Can a girl masturbate?

A: Yes, although it's not believed to be as common as male masturbation.

Q: My girlfriend and I think about boys all the time. I don't admit it to her, but I have these mad fantasies about being with a boy and how it would feel. The problem is, that I daydream so much, sometimes I don't get my homework or my chores done any more. Am I normal?

A: You bet! Especially if you're a young teen. And you're probably more honest than most. Sexual development (puberty) comes rather suddenly for many teenagers, and the sexual feelings that come with it are a shock—exciting, delightful, but hard to deal with in a calm and sensible way. We used to describe what you're feeling as being "boy crazy." It will pass as you get more comfortable with the new you and more used to dealing with boys in a more grown-up way. But for now, try to stay focused on your school work and activities. Spend time with friends and family. Above all, don't get carried away by your feelings or act on them in a way that you'll regret later.

Q: Why are parents so impossible? I'm a high school freshman and I can't date! I can't go to the mall with my friends! I can't buy the clothes or the makeup I want! They think I'll get into trouble if I do what everyone else my age is doing.

A: It does sound like your folks are holding the reins pretty tight. Have you given them any reason to be so strict? Has an older sister or brother gotten into a mess? If neither of these is true, it may be that your parents see all the problems out there and are trying to protect you. Pregnancy, early marriage, sexually transmitted diseases, drug and alcohol misuse, teen auto accidents, suicide—all of these situations might seem remote to you. But, for good reason, they alarm parents who love their children and want only good things for them. So, you need to understand what's behind all of the rules.

Why don't you ask for reasons, and try to hear the feelings behind the words. This may help to reassure your parents about your intentions. I don't think you're being unreasonable in wanting to date, wear makeup, and be with your friends. But you need to accept or at least compromise on the limitations they set for you.

Q: A guy that I'm good friends with keeps talking about how people commit suicide. I'm afraid he's talking about himself, because he's been real down lately. Should I say anything to anyone? Who?

A: Don't delay. Tell a school counselor what you've told me. Maybe there's nothing to it, but many teenagers who kill themselves give out lots of signals, but no one takes it seriously until it's too late. If you're wrong, no harm's been done.

Q: People think I'm cold and stuck up, but I'm really shy. How can I be more friendly? I've never had a date.

A: People who are shy often scare people off because they seem so aloof. One way to dispel this image is to stop thinking about the impression you're making and concentrate hard on what others are saying. Really listen for the meaning of their words. Observe them carefully: how do they look, how are they dressed, how do they feel? All of this can help you take your mind off of yourself and be more natural with others. Try to be yourself; be sincere, be friendly—and don't be afraid to admit that you're feeling shy. It will help people see you as you really are.

Q: What is an orgasm?

A: It's the peak moment of pleasure, normally occurring during sexual intercourse; it can, however, occur outside of intercourse. For the male it is when semen spurts out of the penis. For the woman, it is usually a less focused but very pleasurable experience.

Q: I have a friend who's pregnant and she's a really nice kid, but my mother says I have to stay away from her. Is this fair?

A: Sounds like your Mom is trying to protect you from friends whom she thinks might be a bad example or lead you astray. I don't know your friend, so I can't judge that. But I agree with you that breaking off a friendship only because of a pregnancy isn't a kind thing to do. A teen in trouble needs friends, support, and lots of kindness and understanding. After all, she could have chosen abortion. Instead, she is trying to do the courageous thing: to give her baby life. Try to help your Mom understand this side of it.

Q: Can a woman have sex during her period?

A: Yes, but a heavy menstrual flow and cramping might cause a couple to wait until she is more physically comfortable.

Q: I saw my father naked. He was in the bathroom and I walked in on him. Now I feel so embarrassed and guilty and I keep thinking about how he looked.

A: Your feelings are very normal, including thinking about him. If, as a young woman, you've never seen a man's body before, it's bound to excite your curiosity as well as disturb you a little. Don't dwell on it; get busy with other things, and be yourself with your Dad. He's probably embarrassed too.

Q: My girlfriends and I talk about sex all the time, but we don't know very much. My folks won't answer my questions or else they get all shook up. How can I find some answers?

A: There are books in the library written just for boys and girls your age. Also, you could ask a school counselor for material that answers questions about sex. Why don't you try once more with your parents, explaining that you need to know things and you'd rather hear it from them than from someone else.

Q: My bratty brother got my diary and told my mother what was in it. Now I'm grounded! Don't I have a right to what's mine?

A: You really do, but what did you record that got you into trouble? And was it true? Maybe the grounding has come at the right moment—to save you from worse trouble. If you're doing things that you know are dangerous—drinking, using drugs, making out or having sex—consider the punishment a blessing and thank your mother for caring enough to put her foot down. Chances are, she's trying to protect you from your own inexperience.

As for the privacy bit, when the storm calms, ask your Mom for some house rules to protect you from sibling invasion!

Q: Why do guys have wet dreams?

A: That's really another name for nocturnal emissions, when semen is discharged from the penis at night during sleep. It happens when there's extra, stored-up semen in the boy's body and may occur during a sexy dream.

Part Three

Who I Choose to Be

15~

Being a Woman in Today's World

*I*s there a woman that you really look up to? It might be a rock star or a great Olympic runner, or a television star, or maybe your own grandmother, or the English teacher who helps you out so often. Maybe you admire Mother Teresa, the Catholic nun who for years has worked with the world's poor.

It's really good to find women to admire because they give you a variety of ideas about becoming a woman yourself. You may not necessarily want to be a singer or athlete or a nun, but each one has special qualities that are valuable.

You may pick out certain women because they're unique or far out, or they have wonderful courage or talent or they've overcome big odds to make good. Or maybe they're just so likeable and friendly that you really want to be like them. So you borrow a bit of this and a little of that from all the young and old women you admire. You put them all together and it forms an image of who you'd like to be some day.

This is a great time to be growing up because you have so many options about who and what you hope to become. Never before have young women been able to choose from so many possible careers, lifestyles, and personal qualities. You don't have to limit your choices; you just have to explore the possibilities. But most important, you need to get deeply in touch with your own unique gifts and dreams and let them move you toward your future.

Talking about it with good friends and your parents, praying about it, and staying open to God's will for your life also can help direct you toward the future that is uniquely yours.

Allison gets top grades in high school and she's working to obtain a college scholarship. Her dream is to continue on to law school. Not too many years ago, Allison would have been a rarity, but now women lawyers are commonplace. They've proved they can handle complex legal-business issues and the challenges of the courtroom. Allison hopes to be a criminal attorney and defend poor people accused of crimes. Her mother is encouraging her, even though no one in their family has ever before gone beyond high school.

A classmate, Juanita, is planning a career in medicine and thinks her love for children would make pediatrics a great choice. Despite the long years of training, more and more women are choosing to be doctors. Many specialize in the care of women, babies, or families, but they've also moved into such specialties as surgery and psychiatry.

Denise's father is a career Army man and she has always dreamed of becoming an Army officer, of serving her country and living in far-distant places. The career possibilities in all branches of service are unlimited for women today.

If you visit a police station in any city, you're likely to see a number of female police officers. Television shows with female detectives may not be totally realistic, but a growing number of women now serve in challenging assignments in law enforcement.

Of course, many young women choose more traditional

fields such as teaching, nursing, and social work. All of these make important contributions to people's lives and to society.

Today's educational and career options for women are endless, thanks to women who blazed the trail for the rest of us. We also owe thanks to the women and men who for many years fought for women's rights. We call them feminists, and they waged drawn–out, sometimes bitter battles to break through centuries of prejudice against women. Their goal was to see women accepted as the equals and partners of men.

Of course, the first major step toward equality was back in your grandmother's or great–grandmother's time. Many people campaigned to change the United States Constitution so that women could vote. This was accomplished in 1919 when the 23rd Amendment was passed. Until that time, only men were able to elect the nation's president and the legislators who pass laws at all levels of government.

Over the years, growing numbers of women went to college and began to prove women's abilities in fields once limited to men. In the 1960s, more freedom and opportunity for both blacks and women became an important social cause.

Unfortunately, the bitter controversy over abortion has muddied the issue of woman's equality. Some people insist that "reproductive freedom"—including abortion at will—must be one of their rights. Others, including some who believe in woman's equality, feel so strongly that abortion takes unborn life, they tend to reject not only abortion but the more legitimate rights that women should have.

There continues to be debate, too, about the proper "place" for women. Should women who are wives and mothers work outside the home? Some of the concerns about this are:

- Can a woman make a good home for her husband and family if she also is pursuing a career? Will she have time and energy to prepare meals, deal patiently with family problems, create an environment of warmth and nurturing?

•Will the children be neglected if the mother is gone all day? "Latchkey children" often feel lonely and insecure, returning from school each day to an empty house.

•What will this more worldly role for women do to the relationship between them and their husbands? Many men are threatened by wives who make as much money, perhaps more, than they do. Some resent wives who feel they must work so the family can have luxuries or even necessities.

On the positive side, husbands and fathers might become more active at home if their wives work. Surely, the care of the children and the household belongs to both the woman and the man when both are employed.

More and more homemakers hold outside jobs, usually because the family needs two paychecks or because she is the only parent in the home. But we should be very concerned when mothers who don't need the money work while their children are young, especially under the age of 2.

Psychologists (and perhaps our common sense) tell us that babies and preschool children develop best when the mother, or at least one of the parents, is there each day, holding and cuddling them, feeding and talking and playing with them. When mothers leave them with a babysitter or in an all-day nursery, the bonds between them may not be as strong. Young mothers often learn, to their sorrow, that their little tots grew up while they weren't looking!

Sometimes parents solve the problem by reversing roles. Jake and Melissa decided that Jake, a carpenter, would work at home where he could complete his projects and orders. His wife went to work every morning as a secretary, leaving instructions for their children's care and for starting dinner. Jake enjoyed being with 9-month-old Cheryl and Jonathan, 2. He developed close and loving bonds with them, something some fathers never manage. This isn't everyone's solution, but it works for them.

You can be a good woman even if you break the stereotypes that many people still hold. You can have a career in a non-traditional field; you can work and have babies (maybe not at the same time!); or you can choose not to marry at all and still be a happy and fulfilled woman.

But don't expect any of these choices to be easy. Those women especially who try to be Supermom, Superwife, Superwoman find out that sooner or later they have to compromise. Very few women can be a full-time wife, mother, and career woman, and do an excellent job at all three. Each requires too much time, energy, and commitment. Instead, you might recall the words of Scripture:

> There is an appointed time for everything...
> a time to be born, and a time to die;
> a time to plant, and a time to uproot the plant....

Above all, you should remember one thing: Jesus was the world's biggest supporter of women! When he walked the earth 2000 years ago, women were hardly more than slaves in a culture dominated by men. Yet, Jesus treated women with love and respect. He believed that they were equal to men and he sought their help and support in his ministry.

Jesus defended the woman caught in adultery and challenged the men about their own sinfulness. He met the woman at the well and, although she had a poor reputation, he used her to herald his coming into her town. On Easter morning, it was Mary Magdalene to whom he appeared as the risen Lord, and who confidently announced his resurrection to the skeptical and frightened apostles, huddled together in an upstairs room.

And, of course, it was another Mary who carried him in her womb, gave birth to him, raised him, and who encouraged him to perform his first miracle, at a wedding celebration. She was one of the few persons, men or women, brave enough to stand by the cross when Jesus died.

If there are doubts in your mind about the equality of men and women, these and other examples in Jesus' life should dispel them and give you courage!

Questions for Reflection/Discussion

1. Imagine your "ideal woman." What characteristics does she have? Now imagine the person you would like to be some day.

2. How do you feel about the "women's movement," the struggle to gain full equality between men and women? Can you imagine Jesus as one of its first supporters? What would you say to him about this, if you could?

3. Do you believe it's possible to "have it all," that is, to be homemaker, wife, mother, career woman? If so, why? If not, why not?

16~ Pressures, Pressures Everywhere

We seem to have wandered far afield in the last chapter, going on about career opportunities and women's lib and working mothers. And here you are, just on the verge of young womanhood, with years to go before these might be real issues for you. But it helps to understand these questions now, because you'll hear much pro and con about them as you grow up.

For now, you live in the world of adolescence—and what a world! New friends, perhaps a new school, advanced and interesting new school subjects, all kinds of activities to get into and, of course, your development into womanhood. It's an exciting stage of life. It's also a time that can test you and even tempt you.

Look around you. What do you see? Wonderful things, to be sure: satellite communication bringing us images of far-distant worlds, silver wings that carry us quickly to loved ones far away, medical and scientific procedures which save health and life, computers that play games and do complex calculations in the twinkling of an eye, great music just a dial away, and stores filled with beautiful goods and fresh foods to choose from. What a world we live in!

But not all in the world is good. You live in a culture that makes growing up more complicated than it ever was for your parents or grandparents.

You can see, on television and in nearby towns, neighborhoods that are filled with crime, violence, poverty, pollution, and drug abuse. Growing numbers of teenagers die from drinking and driving and, tragically, from suicide. Alcoholism destroys millions of people and divorce has broken up too many homes. Living, as we do, in a highly populated, affluent, and technological world presents problems that must be solved.

In a society that glorifies personal freedom, there's an attitude out there that says: "What I do is my business and nobody can tell me what to do." Have you heard this before?

People who "do their own thing" think they have no obligation to others. They do what pleases or benefits them, even if it offends or harms someone else—all in the name of personal freedom. So, we read about an angry, disturbed motorist who shoots another driver who cuts him off on the road. We read about drug dealers growing rich by peddling death-dealing substances to teenagers, and pornographers who lure innocent children into making sex films. There are the so-called good citizens who drink then drive, killing others in an accident. And in the name of personal freedom, there are those insisting that their sexual activity is private—but who cause others, including babies, to be infected with the AIDS virus.

Now, freedom is a great thing, but not at someone else's expense. Jesus taught us that we must love others as much as we love ourselves, and that love has to show itself in action, in how we treat those around us.

You may know people who believe that their decisions and actions don't affect anyone but themselves: not their parents, not their brothers or sisters, not their grandparents, not their friends. But that's not true.

Many years ago the poet John Donne wrote, "No man is an island," and by that he meant that each of us and the lives we live affect everyone around us, especially those who love us. We aren't made just for ourselves; we are linked to our family, our community, and the whole human race. What happens to us happens to them. Your family shares the consequences of all the choices that you make, especially when you're young. Some of your most important decisions will involve sexuality.

But the culture's attitude toward sex may make these choices hard. Television, movies, magazines, MTV, rock concerts all foster a cheap and false image of human sexuality. Adults involved in these industries grow rich promoting this image.

If you're an average television viewer, you've been exposed by now to many, many hours of sexually stimulating scenes and suggestive material on daytime and night television. You've listened to talk shows where people openly discuss their sexual affairs outside of marriage. You've heard adults tell teenagers that sex is okay as long as it's "safe" (meaning "use the pill or a condom").

Movie themes no longer deal with simple boy–girl romances. Instead, the focus is more likely to be on casual sex, sexual violence, incest, rape, and some incredibly mindless perversions of what sex is.

If I were a young person growing up today, I would definitely get the message that sexual intercourse is for pleasure only, that it can be used to punish and exploit people, that it's free and intended for everyone, no matter how young or unconnected or uncommitted they are. Most of all, the message comes across that love and commitment really haven't much to do with "making love."

So what has all this got to do with you? Simple, it puts enormous pressure on you to live as a Christian, to respect your body and your God–given sexual nature. It's hard to make good moral choices when all around you, "anything goes." It's hard to live up to your ideals if others think you're weird unless you go right along with the crowd.

Sorry to say, you are going to have to decide your values in a culture that looks on sex as trivial pursuit, as a casual way to have fun or as a sure-fire method for keeping a boyfriend.

This reminds me of a young girl, Darla, who went to an older friend for advice. She told her, "Mickey and I are going to have sex. But we're not going to take any chances. I'm going to take the pill. The problem is, I don't have the money to pay for it every month, and I can't ask my folks—they'd kill me if they knew!"

"Why not make Mickey pay for it?" her friend asked.

"Ask my boyfriend?" Darla asked in a shocked voice. "Why, I don't know him well enough for that!"

Sad. Darla was willing to have sex with a boy that she didn't even feel she knew!

Another reason why you may feel pressured during your teen years has to do with your own growth. A hundred years ago, young people matured sexually much later than they do today. But they married young, often in their teens, and this meant they had sexual interest and feelings for only a rather short time before marrying. But that's changed. The onset of puberty has been going down three months every decade since 1900. Today, boys and girls become sexually mature as early as 10 or 12, some start dating in seventh or eighth grade, go steady at 15, and are permitted unlimited freedom, time, and privacy with their boyfriend or girlfriend. In such a situation, strong sexual feelings grow.

But, while sexual and social development is coming earlier for you, the age of marriage comes later. You're expected and encouraged to wait until you finish school—as late as 22 to 25 years old—before you become a bride. And you will be urged (by your folks and people like me) to remain a virgin until you're married. So you have 10 or more years of sexual maturity in which to remain chaste.

If you really want to live up to this Christian teaching,

you need to face squarely and deal honestly with the pressures of the culture and your peer group during these coming years.

Questions for Reflection/Discussion

1. What attracts you most about the world you live in? What do you like the least?

2. Is it harder to be a teen today than in your parents' time? What are some ways that it might be easier?

3. How, specifically, do your decisions and actions affect other people? Your parents? Your friends? Who else?

4. Do you believe you are, or are not, affected by what you watch on television? What are some ways TV affects you?

~ 17

Holy World, Sinful World: Some Ways We Abuse Sex

Everything that God made is good, including sex. But we human beings, weak and imperfect as we are, sometimes abuse our sexual gifts.

Masturbation Take the case of masturbation, normally more a problem for boys than girls. Masturbation involves touching or rubbing one's sexual organ—the penis or clitoris—to cause intense sexual excitement and possibly orgasm. It is more common for boys than girls because the penis is more obviously external, and because boys are quickly, often strongly, stimulated by sexy visual images. This is not likely to be as true for girls at the same age.

Once there was the mistaken idea that masturbation caused insanity, loss of hair, emotional disturbance, possibly even disease. It was seen as a selfish and perverted act. The church regarded it as a sin because it involved deliberate sexual pleasure outside of marriage.

Today, we know that those earlier fears about the physical or mental effects of masturbation are not true. Masturbation has no impact on a person's health.

We also understand much more about physical and psychological growth into sexual maturity. When a young teen suddenly begins to have sexual urges, she doesn't know quite how to handle these feelings. So, masturbating may become the way that a young person finds to release sexual tension.

The reason doesn't make it right, but the church no longer sees masturbation as a grave sin. There is no reason to burden teenagers with terrible feelings of guilt and shame. Instead, teens need to understand that masturbation may occur as they try to cope with the strong and confused emotions that come with sexual maturing.

The time to worry about masturbation is if it becomes habitual, when it's used casually and repeatedly just to get sexual pleasure. Then it becomes self-centered and an improper use of one's sexual gifts.

But there's another problem with masturbation: it can grow into a habit that causes a teenager to turn into herself for satisfaction, instead of reaching out to other people and toward healthy relationships. It may become, in this case, a symptom of lack of confidence, poor self-esteem, and the person's inability to cope with the challenges of teenage life.

Homosexuality Most of us, as we grow up, become romantically interested in persons of the opposite sex. Eventually, we find one special person whom we love and want to marry. This is hetereosexual behavior and it's the normal way to be. It is how God made humans both for their own pleasure and happiness and for their power to share with God in the making of new life.

As you know, homosexuals are persons attracted to members of their own sex. We think, though no one knows for sure, that in North America about 10 percent of men and 2 percent of women are homosexual.

We do not know what causes homosexuality. Psychologists believe several factors may be involved. Some stress that abnormal development or poor parent relationships in childhood is an important cause. Other theories are that it is inherited, is caused by hormonal imbalance, or that repeated homosexual experiences during teen years may seduce young people into this lifestyle. It's probably safe to say that no person really chooses to be homosexual. There's too many penalties and risks involved.

Sometimes teenagers think they might be homosexual because they have experienced pleasure during masturbation or through an occasional homosexual experience with another person. Or they worry because they have a crush on a teacher or older student, or because they don't fit the stereotype of "masculine" or "feminine."

You need to know that none of the above is an indication of being homosexual. Such thoughts or worries are normal, and so is the doubt you might have about how well you measure up sexually. If you have what seem like serious reasons to think you might be homosexual, talk to a trusted adult (not another teen) to resolve your concern.

It is very wrong to make fun of those who are homosexual or to use such names as "fag," "queer," or "fairy." Homosexuals use the term "gay." As Christians, we are expected to recognize that homosexual persons are children of God and should not be discriminated against in our society.

As we have learned more about homosexuality, it has become harder for the church to say exactly how serious is the guilt involved. The church is very clear that persons who have what is called a homosexual orientation are guilty of no sin at all. This means that if such persons do not engage in sexual activity, they have done no wrong. Those who are active in this way are engaged in wrong behavior. But to be guilty of serious sin, a person must realize the sinfulness of the act and still deliberately do it. Only God can judge the seriousness of the sin.

Sexually Transmitted Diseases More commonly called STDs, these conditions include some that have been around for a long time, but also AIDS.

STDs are communicable diseases that are passed on from an infected person by sexual contact of such body parts as the penis, vagina, rectum, or mouth (this includes French kissing). The following are the most common:

Syphillis It's curable, but only if you know you have it. Estimates are that a half million people in the United States are infected but don't know it. The symptoms begin with a sore on the girl's vagina or inside the vagina or on the boy's penis. The sore may go away, but new symptoms appear: a rash around the sexual organs, low fever, sore throat and glands, sometimes loss of hair. These symptoms also will disappear, but in the final stage of syphillis, the heart and brain are damaged and the person may die. Unless treated, syphillis will last a lifetime. A person may unknowingly get the disease in teen years and later pass it on to their wife or husband, or an unborn child.

Gonorrhea Sexual intercourse is the chief way to get this disease, sometimes called clap. If a girl gets gonorrhea, she will, if she's lucky, get a slight discharge from the vagina and experience a burning feeling during her period, but she may also become infertile or experience lifelong pelvic pain. Eighty percent of infected girls will have no symptoms at all. Because there are often no symptoms and because there are no foolproof tests, many people never know they have the disease. A pregnant woman with gonorrhea may give birth to a blind baby. This disease usually can be cured with penicillin.

Herpes II This is incurable and it is believed that some 20 million Americans have it. It causes sores in the sexual area or rectum, sometimes on the mouth. These are very painful and easily spread. An unborn baby can get the disease from an infected mother and may even die from it. Herpes II is a serious matter.

AIDS You probably have heard a lot of frightening stories about AIDS, not all of it true. Here are some facts: AIDS was first diagnosed in 1981. There are between 30,000 and 50,000 cases today, but it's estimated there may be as many as one and a half million by the early 1990s. The disease, which is incurable, has caused thousands of deaths. It is transmitted through sexual contact, contaminated needles in drug use, and through contaminated needles used in receiving blood transfusions. When giving blood, new sterilized needles are always used.

Ninety percent of those infected are homosexual men and/or drug users. However, the number of heterosexual persons with AIDS may increase in the next few years. Women can be infected through sexual contact with bi-sexual men (those with both same-sex and opposite-sex partners). Persons have contracted AIDS because needles used in blood transfusions were contaminated. And some babies have been born with the disease because their mothers were infected.

What are we to think about AIDS victims morally? Some people will tell you that God is punishing homosexuals and drug users by giving them AIDS. How could this be, since innocent people, including children and babies, also can get AIDS? The church teaches that sexual activity is right only within marriage and that homosexual activity is wrong. But it has refused to see AIDS as punishment. Instead, it has tried to respond to suffering people as Jesus did. In many places around the country, church agencies have set up AIDS counseling and care centers.

The church has argued for just treatment of AIDS sufferers because many such persons have lost their jobs, their homes, and their standing in the community. Often, friends and families have deserted them. Instead, we are called as Christians to be compassionate and caring, just as Jesus cared for lepers in his time.

Rape In simplest terms, rape is when a man forces a woman to have sexual relations with him against her will. It is a terrible deed, most often done by persons who have great hostility and violence inside of them. Most of them are emotionally ill people who achieve satisfaction by inflicting themselves on a helpless victim. In a real sense, violent rape is not so much "sexual" as it is an act of cruel violence.

There is another form of rape you may know about. It isn't the violent attack of a stranger on a dark street but happens with someone you know as a friend or acquaintance. It's called date-rape. The sad thing is that many young people don't recognize it as rape at all.

The boy doesn't use a knife or a gun to make the girl give in, but he may use physical force and a lot of verbal harrassment. And, if challenged, he probably would justify it by saying that she teased him, "led him on," or said she wanted sex, then refused.

Some girls also wouldn't call it rape, because somehow they have the wrong idea that they owe a boy whatever he wants because he took her out and spent money on her. Both girls and boys sometimes justify date-rape by claiming that males can't control their sexual passion.

An Ann Landers column recently reported a survey which asked 11- to 14-year-old students their views about rape. Here are some of their answers:

• Half of the students thought a woman who walks alone at night and/or dresses seductively is "asking to be raped."

• Sixty-five percent of boys and 47 percent of girls said it is okay for a man to force a woman to have sex if they have been dating more than six months.

• Thirty-one percent of boys and 32 percent of girls believed it was acceptable for a man to rape a woman who has had previous sexual experiences with him.

All of these views are pure nonsense! The fact is that no person *ever* has the right to force another person into a sexual act, no matter what the circumstances. Even married people haven't got that right!

As a young woman, you need to know this, and to protect yourself in every way that you can:

• By avoiding dark, deserted, or unsafe parts of town. Don't jog by yourself; don't walk home alone from babysitting; don't ever accept a ride from anyone you don't know well.

• By being careful whom you date and where you go on

the date. (Remember, secluded places are always a risk).

• By stating very clearly, if a boy pressures you, that you don't want sex and that he could be criminally prosecuted if he persists.

• By being conscious of your own behavior, language and dress, so that boys can't get the wrong impression of your intentions.

Incest This means that the sexual violation has happened with a relative. You read in an early chapter about Tanya, an 11-year-old, whose uncle seduced her by first showing her affection, then climbed into her bed and had sex with her. Because he was her uncle, Tanya didn't know how to react. She knew instinctively that what he was doing was wrong, but she was afraid to tell anyone because she thought she was responsible.

Incest happens mostly to girls, but it also can happen to boys. It is done to children of all ages, from toddlers through teenagers. Seldom does it happen only once, as in rape, but usually goes on for months or years.

It's terrible, not only because it is sexual abuse, but also because the child is so vulnerable. This is a relative whom she trusts, but who takes advantage of her. As with Tanya, she may feel deep shame and guilt. Such children need professional help to heal the psychological damage done to them.

Abortion No doubt you have heard a lot about abortion from friends, your family, in the classroom, or on television. It's a very complicated and important issue because it involves the lives of women, their babies, their families, and the whole legal structure of the society we live in.

Every day in the United States, more than 4,000 unborn babies die from abortion—nearly one and a half million every year. Unfortunately, some laws permit abortion on demand and some women, who would never do it illegally, think this makes abortion morally all right. They figure, "If it's legal, it must be moral."

Abortions take place for many reasons: because women

feel they can't afford a baby, or think they're too old or too young to have a child, or they don't want a child because it's inconvenient, or they already have other children and don't want more. Sometimes, poor health is involved, even though most doctors today say that treating the mother's illness and letting the pregnancy continue is less risky than an abortion.

Also, some women and young girls have abortions because they are unmarried. They are panic-stricken or embarrassed or scared, or they're pressured by a boyfriend or parent to end the pregnancy.

It is sad that many women who get abortions don't know what abortion really is. They have heard that it doesn't really kill anything; it just removes a little bit of tissue from their body. They don't know—no one has ever told them—how very human the growing little baby is inside their bodies.

Abortion truly does kill a tiny but perfectly formed baby whose life began when the father's sperm cell joined the mother's egg cell. Take a minute to go back to Chapter 3 to read again about your fantastic nine months of life before birth.

The medical science of fetology (from *fetus,* which means "offspring") can now treat a baby before it is born. It can do tests, perform surgery, and measure the vital signs and health of a developing but unborn child. Maybe you have seen the amazing photograph of a baby sucking its thumb while still curled inside its mother. If this is not human and living, what is?

The fact is, then, that abortion kills this new little life by sucking it out of the mother's body with a vacuum tool or by scraping it out with a curved knife. That's an ugly thing to think about or imagine, but that is what happens.

From the very beginning, the Catholic church has taught that to kill an unborn child is an immoral act. The church reminds us that God created all life; each of us belongs to God. Our lives are precious gifts and we have no right to take our own lives nor to kill another person. To destroy the precious and innocent life of a newly developing baby is a great evil.

This doesn't mean that the church cares only about the unborn child. Just being against abortion isn't enough. We also must want to help the distressed pregnant woman who thinks abortion will solve her problem.

Women in poor health should be guaranteed good medical care. Those unhappy because they are pregnant need to know that often it is their own physical condition that causes their feelings. After the baby arrives, negative feelings most often change to joy and delight. If not, adoption is possible: There are thousands of childless couples waiting for a newborn child that they may adopt.

Free pre-natal care and counseling, better housing, and job opportunities are needed by poor families. And young teenagers should be treated with care and love, helped to understand all the alternatives they have, and given the chance to continue their education and their life, during and after their pregnancy.

There is no easy answer to all difficult situations. But killing unborn children is a terrible response to the problem. Jesus helped people in all sorts of difficulties, but he never solved a problem by taking someone's life. He restored life and gave people love and hope. How about you?

Pornography If you've read this far in the chapter, you may be feeling rather depressed by now. We've dealt with a whole lot of unpleasant facts that depict sex in a sordid way. Pornography is the last topic we'll discuss, but it's important because it's related to some of the other issues.

What really is pornography? Is it dirty books? Nude women? Sexy dancers? A couple on television having sex? The answer to all of the above is yes...and no. Confused? That's because our society has become so open about sexuality that the old meanings have been blurred.

We accept, now, that sexuality is a significant part of life; therefore it is not wrong to depict it in the arts. We acknowledge that the human body is one of God's beautiful creations; therefore nudity is not automatically bad. It just depends on how sexual themes are shown—and why.

In simplest terms, pornography is material that is very sexually explicit and is intended to sexually arouse people. It is a multi-million dollar business that includes "adults only" bookstores and theaters showing "skin flicks." But now pornography has reached into our homes with X-rated cable television, hard rock video, and even telephone systems with obscene messages for the callers.

Violent pornography is seen by many people as the worst type: porn that links sexual activity with violence, such as rape scenes and brutal sexual acts. According to a national panel of experts, this kind of material causes people who look at it or read it to become more aggressive and actually more likely to commit violent acts.

Another terrible form of pornography involves children. Pornographers entice very young children as well as teens into sexual activity so they can take photographs or make films to sell. This experience often causes lifelong damage to the children involved.

But what many adults worry about most is the effect that pornography can have on people who get immersed in it. Pornography distorts the meaning that God has given to sexuality. It suggests that sex isn't fun unless it's violent, that sex can be enjoyed without any feeling for the other person, that a woman is a thing to be used, that children are fair game. We often hear of sexual crimes committed by individuals who say they got the idea from a movie or porno book. Many young people look at sexually stimulating material out of curiosity. But they need to know that if you take bad food into your mouth, your body will be poisoned; if you take spoiled messages into your mind and heart, your soul will be poisoned.

Questions for Reflection/Discussion

1. Are you surprised by the church's teaching in this chapter? Is the church too easy on any issues? Too hard?

2. Do you know anyone who is homosexual? How do you feel about this person? Does the church help you to be more understanding?

3. How should people treat those with AIDS? How would you act if a classmate got AIDS?

4. Specifically, what would you do if you were date-raped? Do you believe forced intercourse is ever okay? Why? Why not?

5. Think of five steps you can take to protect yourself from physical assault.

6. Reflect on what you know about abortion. What are your deepest feelings about it?

7. Are you convinced that pornography is sinful? If so, why? If not, why not?

18~

Sex According to Jesus

Here's good news for you! The Catholic church, which began almost 2000 years ago, thinks more highly of sex than does popular television or your crowd of friends! The church is not against sex.

I'd better explain that, because some teens (and adults, too) really believe that people who are "religious" also are narrow-minded and negative about sexuality. It is true that Christian religions haven't always stressed the goodness of human sexuality. Your parents—or more likely, your grandparents—may have grown up feeling guilty because, as normal human beings, they had thoughts and feelings and curiosity about sex. They may have been embarrassed by their sexual bodies.

Their guilt stems from a long tradition in the world and in the church, when people didn't understand sex all that well. They were afraid of it. Christian leaders, including writers, expressed fears that being sexual could keep a person from being holy also. In fact, many Christians thought that being a virgin dedicated to God was superior to living their lives as sexually active married persons.

It's also true that women were badly treated at the time of Christianity's beginnings. They were seen as inferior, and some church officials warned that women would keep men from living holy lives by tempting them into sexual sin.

It wasn't like that with Jesus. He treated women as equals, defended them, even when others attacked them. Jesus had friendships with many women. They supported him in his holy life.

Furthermore, Jesus was truly a male person—though he was God. He experienced the same growth and development as boys that you know. Like all young men, he experienced the same curiosity, feelings, and sexual urges that all males do. That's one of the things we mean when we say that Jesus was "fully human." In other words, he was a sexed person with a male character and personality. And he was fully sexual, but he did not marry nor engage in sexual activity.

The example of Jesus is one of the reasons why so much has changed in attitudes toward sexuality. We have come to appreciate it as God's gift, as a valuable part of being human. The old ideas about sexuality being a dangerous or dirty thing are no longer accepted by most Christians.

If you believe in Jesus and want to be his follower, you can do nothing more important than by *celebrating* your sexuality. Here are some ways to do this:

1. Really believe that being a sexual person is a wonderful thing.

• Sexuality is something you *are,* not something you do. It is your way of being, to the world and to other people.

• God has given us our bodies and they are beautiful creations—beautiful in how they work...in the feelings they give us (including sexual)...in their power to create new life.

2. Understand and respect your sexual self.

• Sex is not a toy, or just a means of pleasure, but a power to communicate deep feeling to others.

• God designed sexual intercourse as a symbol of a total gift between a man and woman.

• Sexual intercourse is an act that has many consequences: physical, emotional, spiritual, and social.

• Sexual intercourse is a human act, potentially very good but which sometimes is abused by people who do not use it as an expression of love.

• Sexual intercourse is only going to be as good as the couple's total relationship. Without commitment, emotional bonding, faithfulness, and deep feelings of trust and love, sex is not truly satisfying and is without meaning. That means that a commited relationship—marriage—is the context for sex that God planned from the beginning.

3. Realize that people are more important than pleasure.

• Jesus showed us how to live the principle that love is the single most important concern for a Christian. He challenges us to ask, What is the truly loving thing to do in this situation, for myself? For this other person? For those who care about me and are responsible for me?

4. Reach "authentic freedom" in sexuality.

• To be authentic means to be genuine, to be able to believe enough in yourself that you can accept and integrate your sexuality into your total personality.

• It means being free enough from pressure that you can decide on your own sexual style, your own way of being a woman, based on your own vision and personal values and in your own best interests. It also means having the freedom and power to say no as well as yes.

5. Establish a direction for yourself.

• This means faithfully keeping the ideal of sexual chastity, even though you will also want to accept your own humanness and failure. It is not a good idea, since it serves no purpose, to agonize over "What did I do?" if you did something you're ashamed of, or even if you think you have committed sin. Instead, you need to seek reconciliation, and to ask yourself, often and always, "Where am I going...and growing? Am I becoming the person I want to be? Am I still trying to stay faithful to my principles?" As human beings, we will not always be successful, but we must always try to be faithful. This is how God will judge us.

6. Value your reproductive powers and the gift of parenthood.

To do this, even at this early point in your life, try to appreciate and understand the gift that God gives us in our sexuality. We can cooperate with God in bringing new life into the world. Here are some ideas about that:

- Bringing children into the world is an act of hope, faith, and optimism. Jesus loved little children and warned against anyone who would abuse them. Even when he was tired and busy, he said, "Let the little children come to me."
- Being parents helps a couple to become more caring and loving people. While it is true that children require much work, they also bring enjoyment and deep satisfaction to a married couple. Just ask your parents!

Questions for Reflection/Discussion

1. How do you and your parents differ on sexual issues? Why do you think this is so? What might you do about this?

2. Would you like to have known Jesus? Imagine a meeting with him. What questions would you ask him?

3. How do you truly feel about being a sexual person? What is good about your sexuality? Are there bad aspects? If so, what are they?

19~

Making My Own Decisions

How do you make up your mind about things? Let's suppose you're studying for a hard science test that will determine your final grade. The phone rings and it's your friend Tammy. "Come to the game with me," she says. Now, basketball is your favorite sport and Tammy is your best friend. But grades are important too. You promised your Dad you'd bring up your science mark to a B. So you have to decide: "Do I go to the game with my friend or do well on the test and please my father." As often happens, two good values conflict with each other.

Maybe you decide to slam the book shut and take off for the gym. Or you regretfully tell Tammy, "Sorry, maybe next time." Or you might compromise: study for a good period of time, and then meet your friends for pizza after the game.

Some people find it very easy to make even hard decisions. They simply do what they feel like doing, regardless of the values involved or the consequences that might result. For instance, Pete wants a pair of the latest Adidas running shoes—very expensive. So he harasses his mother until he gets them, even though the family really can't afford to pay that much for them.

Homemaker Adele Jones is left off the invitation list for a neighborhood party. Angry and hurt, she forbids her children to play with the kids whose parents snubbed her. In both cases, feelings dictated the choice made.

We know that feelings are an important part of being human. Joy, sadness, pity, anger, hope, sympathy, love—all of these and many other emotions are what make life interesting and exciting.

Feelings are useful, too. They can suggest when a decision might be good or bad. If you went to the basketball game even though you were failing science, your feelings of guilt and anxiety might convince you to leave the game at half-time to go home and hit the books. The warm feeling you get when you do a special favor for Grandma encourages you to other good acts.

But choices can't be based only on emotion. You also must use your reason and your will in decision making.

Reason is the thinking, the logic, the values, and the loving care you call into play as you sort out a decision. Will is the determination and the power that you have inside of you to follow through on what you know is the right thing to do. Even when it's hard.

Let's say you want to be a doctor, but each time you're given a chance to take honors classes, you turn it down. You know it means extra work, and there are so many fun things you'd rather do. Also, deep down you're afraid you might not measure up to the harder courses. So you pass over the chance to prepare well for your future.

How intelligent is this decision? If you're taking the easy way now, how will you cope with the bigger challenges ahead? You pass up an opportunity to prepare well for your future. One decision builds on another, and from this you develop habits of decision making that can be smart or not wise at all.

Values are possibly the most important test of a good decision. Is your decision based on values that matter to you? Even though you might be dying to go to the movies with your friends, can you responsibly go if you promised to keep an eye on your little sister? Are you being fair? Are you acting selfishly, breaking a promise?

How loving is your decision? You may think you're showing love by lying to your parents to cover your brother coming home at 4 AM. But if you're truly concerned about what's good for him, maybe you should consider that he might be getting into some bad habits, possibly drinking or drug use. Maybe he needs Mom and Dad's guidance instead of your cover-up.

In other words, you need to use all of your thought and emotion to make decisions. You have to look at an important issue in the light of how you feel about it, how it will affect you, how it will affect those around you, especially those you love.

After you've applied your own intelligence to make a good decision, you then need to pray about it. Jesus sends us the Holy Spirit for just such situations, to give us help with hard choices. If you pray, asking the Spirit for wisdom, you can feel confident that your decision will be a good one. Or you might realize, after prayer, that your first choice wasn't the best, that you need to find an alternative.

What sorts of things are worth praying about? Whatever matters in your life deserves prayer: what to study in school, a choice of friends, problems in the family, and any other situation that concerns you. Most of all, you need to ask for God's help when the choice involves moral behavior. Sexuality is such an issue.

Making decisions is much more complicated than most people realize. And decision making changes as you mature. Psychologists say there are three basic ways people make up their minds about important matters. They call these "levels of moral decision making."

Level One Choices are based mostly on fear or pleasure.

Persons who make decisions at this level act according to whether they are afraid of being punished or are hoping for some sort of pleasure.

Six-year-old Karen doesn't raid the cookie jar because she knows, if caught, she'll be spanked or deprived of dessert. Phil, 11, takes a 40-minute shower because he enjoys it, although his sister will have to wash her hair in cold water. Jerry and Jan make out at a party even though they don't really care about each other, but it feels so good.

All young children and many adults make choices based solely on fear or pleasure. Mature people do not.

Level Two Decisions made at this level are for the sake of rules and laws or a desire to look good. Persons conform to the laws of society, parental rules, or the expectations of friends, no matter what they may think themselves.

Tom goes to Mass on Sunday, not because he wants to pray or participate, but because his father told him to. Another person, Mr. Jackson, divorced from his wife, sends her scarcely enough money to support their children, though he can afford more. He does so strictly to stay within the law.

Bonnie, white, and Conrad, black, have a great friendship. But most of the neighborhood where Bonnie lives thinks such relationships are "bad." Bonnie is looked down on and she finally decides to break off the friendship to live up to her community's belief about keeping the races separate.

Typically, school-age children are very much into this "law and order" stage, but many adults also never get beyond it.

Level Three Here, decisions are made according to significant values, that is, they're based on a person's principles instead of simple feelings or rule-keeping.

One example might be Donella, who knows she's forbidden to go down to the old quarry. One day, as she walks to school, she hears a child's cry. Thinking someone might be trapped in the rough quarry bed, she disobeys her mother and runs down into the pit. There is a little four year old, and Donella is able to pull her out of danger. She has gone beyond a rule to a value-based act: to rescue a child in trouble.

Many young men went to jail rather than fight in the Vietnam war based on a significant value: refusing to kill in a war they regarded as unjust.

It is sometimes hard to act on Christian principles. Often, the values expressed in the Catholic faith differ from those that our society upholds, especially in sexual issues. Here is where you feel the pressure to conform to the "popular" thinking.

Here are eight simple steps for good decision making:

1. Be very clear about what it is that you must decide. Name the issue or problem. It may help you to write it down.

2. Decide: What do I want to accomplish or to see happen, whichever decision I make?

3. Figure out all the issues and factors involved. Get the facts accurately, and don't duck any of them.

4. Think of the principles that Jesus puts in front of you: to do the loving thing for self and others, to respect your own and others' feelings. To be honest with yourself and all other persons, to be fair and just. How do these apply in this particular issue?

5. Figure out all possible decisions you could make and list the risks and advantages of each one.

6. As you begin to sense the choice you'd like to make, carefully check out your motives, asking yourself, Why do I want to do this? Do I really want to?

7. Give yourself a little time for prayer and reflection. Never mind talking to God. God knows what's in the works. Let God talk to you.

8. Finally, decide what seems like the best alternative. Then follow through on it, using lots of "will power" and asking God's help.

Naturally, you wouldn't go through all this for simple

decisions, such as which color skirt to buy or whether to have pizza or a cheeseburger for lunch. You would save this process for those complicated things that really matter to you. Spend a moment right now, and jot down six important issues where you might have to make decisions that are important to your life.

Questions for Reflection/Discussion

1. Are you afraid to make decisions that go against your family's views? Against your friends'? Who should be the final decision maker?

2. Which is harder for you: to make an important decision, or to live up to it afterward? Why do you think this is so?

3. Where do you think you are on the three Levels of Decision Making? Give reasons or examples for your answer. What are two things you can add to your decision-making process?

20~ The Good News of Saying No

One of the most important decisions you'll ever make is deciding to remain a virgin until you marry. Maybe this surprises you. You feel that you wouldn't really need to make a conscious decision; it's a foregone conclusion you would never have sex before marriage.

Or, on the other side, perhaps you think the decision is easy because having sex is no big deal. You know lots of boys and girls who get sexually involved, some without much thought and they don't take it all that seriously. For them, sex is just a fun activity that doesn't require love, commitment, or a big struggle of conscience. So, you might believe they're right.

Take a serious look now at some possible consequences of having a sexual relationship before marriage. Let us consider these through the stories of five young people very much like yourself.

The Broken Love Affair Everyone at Eastside High agreed that Adam and Kathy were the perfect couple. He was the class president; she was a cheerleader; both were on the honor roll. They planned to attend college together. Someday, they said, they'd get married.

They spent all their spare hours together, often at Kathy's house, and gradually their love became more and more physical. Finally, although they had promised one another it wouldn't happen, they had sexual intercourse. At first, it was wonderful, but soon they began to quarrel: What if their folks found out? Was it a sin? What if Kathy got pregnant? Was a condom enough protection? Should Kathy take the pill? Could they, should they, sneak off and get married and not tell anyone?

Kathy decided they had to stop having sex; the worry and guilt was too much for her. Mark felt guilty too, but also angry. If she loved him, how could they separate now? They argued more and more. Kathy accused Mark of using her; Mark said Kathy was betraying him and their love. After one especially painful argument, they broke up.

Now both are dating other people, but they still bear grief and regret in their hearts. They both wonder: How could a love that seemed so "right" go wrong? Why did they lose their great hope for happiness? *Premature sex can break up even the most genuine love relationship.*

Marked for Life Sixteen-year-old Sarah didn't date much. She was nice looking and a good student, but very shy. At the start of her junior year in high school, Sarah met Lenny, a senior, who put on a big rush with phone calls, Saturday night dates, and, finally, his class ring.

Naive and inexperienced, Sarah was madly infatuated by Lenny's sweet words of love and his masculine aggressiveness. Within a few weeks, they were having sex. Suddenly, in the third month of the relationship, Lenny stopped asking Sarah out, didn't answer her phone calls, avoided her in the hall. One day, she saw him holding hands with a senior girl. Clearly, it was all over. Sarah was devastated, but gradually, she began getting out again.

One morning, as she dressed, Sarah noticed a couple of

sores in her vaginal area. One had broken open and was very painful. When the sores didn't heal and more appeared, Sarah went to see her family's doctor. To her horror, she learned that she had herpes II, a disease contracted in sexual contact. She knew it came from Lenny because he was the only sexual partner she had ever had. The doctor told her he knew of no cure for herpes II. He also said that if she were to have a baby, the child would possibly be born with the disease. Sarah now prays daily that medical science will find a cure for her condition. *Each year, 2.5 million teenagers become infected with a sexually transmitted disease (STD).*

The "Honorable" Thing to Do Pam and Dave dated from their first year of high school on. In April of their senior year, Pam discovered she was pregnant, even though they had used contraceptives off and on. At first, they talked about abortion, but Pam couldn't bring herself to do it.

One painful night, they told their families. Their parents were shocked and upset. There was only one solution, they said: Dave and Pam must get married! So, two weeks after graduation, a small, quiet wedding took place. To save money, the newlyweds moved in with his folks. Dave's plans for college were scrapped and he got a job in a processing plant. Pam worked in a fast food store.

When Pam gave birth to an 8-pound boy, she left her job to take care of him. At first things went well, but slowly Pam began to hate living with Dave's family, sharing a bathroom with younger kids, never having privacy for herself and Dave, and—especially—listening to his mother tell how to bring up her baby. Pam missed her friends and the enjoyable times they used to have. "I'm only 18 and all I do is work!" Dave felt trapped, too. He remembered his dream of becoming an accountant. His resentment toward his job and his wife ("who got me into this") grew, as it did even toward little Michael, whom he loved dearly.

After months of fighting, Pam and Dave went to a counselor who told them they weren't ready for marriage. They decided divorce was the only answer. Pam moved back with her folks and is trying now to raise the baby alone. David entered the state university. He visits his son whenever he comes home, but he and Pam still blame each other for the way things turned out. *When teenagers marry because of pregnancy, nine out of ten marriages end up in divorce. There are too many pressures, not enough maturity, and they need to continue their own growing up.*

A Price to Pay Elizabeth was a pretty and popular 15 year old, but she loved to party. One night someone offered her a joint and she got her first "high" on marijuana. It was exciting and different and she went back for more. Gradually, Elizabeth moved into a fast crowd that drank and used pot and had sex freely, stimulated by the drugs and liquor. Elizabeth didn't really enjoy the sex, but she was caught up in the excitement of doing forbidden things.

By 16, she had been dropped by her old friends who had watched the change in her. The fast crowd still welcomed her, but Elizabeth had begun to regret her past deeds. She knew now that she didn't want to be part of this any more. But, unfortunately, she now had a reputation as an "easy mark" and only certain boys wanted to go out with her. Some of them pretended they had had sex with her even though it wasn't true.

Today, Elizabeth is a high school junior and she is still trying to make up for the bad and foolish things she did. She is determined to start over again, to win back the respect and friendships she once had, but she is often lonely and alone. *A bad reputation is hard to live down, especially for a girl.*

Deadly Decision When Joyce and Chris met, it was instant love! Right from the start, they were inseparable at school and spent evening after evening together. They tried to study but had to struggle to keep their hands off each other. After a while, they began to have sex.

Both of them came from very strict Catholic homes and

they didn't want to risk a pregnancy or have their parents find out, so Joyce took the pill whenever she could get it. But she got pregnant anyway. They knew their parents would be furious, so, in panic, Joyce arranged for an abortion. She was reassured, "It's only a piece of tissue; it will be gone before you know it."

It was over easily and quickly—except for the nightmares that Joyce began to have. She had seen pictures of unborn babies in her health class at school. She kept visualizing how her baby might look at each stage of the pregnancy (even though that pregnancy had ended).

She stopped going to Communion and told Chris that she couldn't forgive him for pushing her into killing her baby. She wonders how she can ever hold up her head again. Though he suffers less, Chris is also filled with remorse. He wonders if God will punish them for the sin they committed. *Last year, one million teenage girls got pregnant. Of these, 400,000 aborted their unborn children and many now suffer great guilt and loss of self-respect.*

The consequences are clear: Having sex can hurt you in many ways, changing your life, ending your dreams, shutting off your spiritual and intellectual growth, destroying your parents' faith and trust in you. Saying "no" to sex is the wisest and most moral decision a young person can make!

But don't expect it to be easy. You live in a culture that makes sexual activity very enticing. So you need to know for sure what you believe and why you believe it. You need to recognize chastity as a great value, as something that is good for you and your future life. And you need to act in a way that supports your intention to remain a virgin.

You can do this in many specific ways:

1. Carefully choose your friends. Choose among those who have high standards and dreams, who value themselves and their sexuality, who believe as you do. Don't think you can reform the others.

2. Avoid dangerous situations and temptations. Don't park, don't date alone night after night. If you end up in a dark, secluded place with someone you care for, get out of there as fast as you can!

3. Make concrete plans for fun things to do. When you make a date, work together, for example, on a school committee, go to sports events, the early movie, dances, picnics, take your kid brother to the zoo. Go to church together, join the youth group. Do fun things with other people.

4. Don't pet. Hugging and kissing feels wonderful, but it builds up a desire for more and more intimacy. As a girl, you need to know that by their very nature, boys become sexually aroused faster than girls do when "making out." You may be feeling only very affectionate, but your boyfriend may be approaching passion. That fire, built up by prolonged kissing and fondling, can cause teens with very good intentions to get carried away.

5. Refuse to drink or use drugs, and expect your date to do the same. These can be lethal to good intentions because they cause you to lose inhibitions and a sense of personal resolve. And of course, drinking is a leading cause of death on the highway.

6. Wear clothes that put the emphasis on you as a whole person. Clothes give messages about the wearer. A girl (or boy, for that matter) advertises her values by how she dresses. Super-sexy clothing and makeup—minis, revealing sweaters, skin-tight jeans, whatever focuses attention on the body—puts ideas in the boy's mind that you are interested in sex.

7. Express your intentions by how you communicate. Modest language tells people what a person is. So, too, do dirty stories, vulgar language, or sexually suggestive comments, even though they might be used to impress others. If you give boys this message, they may expect you to live up to it. *Never* permit a date to bring in pornographic magazines or videos.

8. Be ready with a response if you are pressured to have sex. There are many possible answers to many possible "lines" that boys use. Here are a few of them:

Boy: "If you really loved me, you'd say yes."

Girl: "If you really loved me, you wouldn't pressure me."

Boy: "I just don't understand—why won't you do it?"

Girl: "I don't understand why you keep asking. I've made a decision: No sex until marriage."

Boy: "You say you love me; how could it be wrong to make love?"

Girl: "I think you're terrific and I really care. But sex for me means total commitment, and we just aren't there yet."

Boy: "I'm so crazy about you. I just can't wait any longer!"

Girl: "I'm sorry; you'll have to find another girl because I'm going to wait."

Boy: "You know I'll respect you and love you after we have sex. Nothing will change."

Girl: "Maybe it won't for you, but it will for me. I'll lose my respect for myself, and that matters to me."

Boy: "You look so beautiful and I feel so romantic. Getting together would make everything perfect."

Girl: "I feel romantic too, but I'm not looking for perfection. I'll settle for a few hugs and a kiss."

Boy: "I've got protection. What are you afraid of?"

Girl: " I'm afraid of people who try to make me do things I don't want to do. And I don't want to have sex."

There are other good answers. You might want to figure out a few of your own. The key is to know that you are going to say no.

But sometimes girls, especially the young and inexperienced, are afraid to turn a boy down because they fear they will lose him. The truth is, if a boy really cares about a girl as a person, not just a sex toy, he will be more interested than ever when she says "no sex."

Seventeen-year-old Joe put it this way, "Sharon told me to back off, and—though I didn't admit it to her—I was glad. My pride was a little hurt, but I know I'm really not ready for a sexual relationship. I guess I thought maybe she expected it."

Kurt, a popular athlete, said he liked his girl better than ever because, "She's got confidence in herself. She knows she doesn't have to have sex to keep me interested. I want someone like that."

Some boys admit they get mad or embarrassed if a girl turns them down, but they say it depends on how she does it. Pete stopped asking Laura out, not because she said no, but because she laughed at him and made him feel stupid. But Tom insists, "If a girl still acts sweet to me, I feel stronger toward her than ever."

Of course, there are some teenagers who may not handle rejection that way. If your "no" causes a boy to pull out of the relationship, as painful as it may be, he isn't worth crying over. He probably did not care about you in the way that you deserve. That doesn't make him bad, but self-centered and immature.

Most of all, you need to believe that you are *not* a sex object to be used, but a beautiful person to be valued.

Questions for Reflection/Discussion

1. Which story in this chapter stands out? Why?

2. Have you made a definite commitment to remain a virgin until marriage? What are the reasons for your decision?

3. Besides the ideas in this chapter, are there other ways to say no? Share these with a friend. Ask a boy you trust what he thinks.

4. Reflect before answering: "Are you afraid to say no?" If you are, search for the reasons.

21~ It Will Never Happen to Me

That's what just about every girl says when someone warns her that sex may lead to pregnancy. No one believes getting pregnant will happen to them. But, as you know from the last chapter, every year at least a million teenage girls become pregnant out of marriage. They then have to face certain choices, and none of them are easy. A girl named Kimberly wants to tell you her story.

Hi. My name is Kimberly, but my friends call me Kim. I'm 18 years old, but I feel a lot older because a lot of things have happened to me.

I think I was a pretty typical kid. I grew up in a nice house with a brother and two sisters and my parents and a cat named Muffin. I was always a pretty good student and had lots of friends.

At the end of my sophomore year, I met Scott. He

was a junior and just the neatest guy, like he was cute and tall and had a darling smile. I was crazy about him right from the start. He liked me too, and we were a pair right away.

That summer between my sophomore and junior year was wonderful. Scott and I did everything together and we had so much fun. I knew I loved him, and one night at an outdoor movie, he told me he loved me.

At first my parents, especially Dad, thought we were seeing too much of each other, but they got to like him a lot, and when we decided to go steady, they didn't say too much, except Mom thought I should date other guys too, just for experience, you know.

But I couldn't do that. They just didn't understand how close we were. By fall, we were starting to think that maybe this is it! Maybe we're meant for each other. We decided that we'd go to the same college and maybe we'd get married in school without anyone knowing it. Everything was perfect, but we didn't tell our folks because we knew they'd say we were "too young." I don't know...maybe they were right.

Well, pretty soon we got very involved physically and one night we finally went all the way. Maybe it's not like this with everyone, but it was beautiful! I loved him and I knew he loved me. I felt guilty, a little, but I thought: How could it be wrong when we feel like we do? We were committed to each other.

You might be surprised to know that we didn't have sex real often...only when we just needed each other so much...and when we could do it without any chance of being discovered.

Then one day, about seven months after we first started going together, I realized my period was late. I was never late, so I noticed it. But I didn't worry because I had a cold and I thought it might be that. I don't know why Scotty and I never worried about me getting pregnant. I guess we just didn't think it would happen. Anyway, the way we felt, it didn't seem like the worst thing that could happen.

But by the time I had skipped my period altogether, I panicked. I went to a counselor at school and she sent me to a clinic where they test you for pregnancy. I couldn't believe it when they told me I was pregnant! I cried. I kept asking the doctor, Couldn't the test be wrong? And he kept saying in a nice way: no. After a few days of worrying, I told Scott. He didn't say anything for a long time. He just kept shaking his head and saying real low, "God."

We talked and talked and talked, mostly about getting an abortion. We knew how hard our folks would take the pregnancy. And we felt so guilty and bad. But I guess we knew we'd never do that. This was a baby that we made and how could we kill it? But we just couldn't bring ourselves to tell our parents. I guess I knew that eventually we'd have to.

I started getting sick in the morning, and one day Mom found me throwing up in the bathroom. I told her I had the flu and I stayed home from school. But things got worse and worse and finally I told Mom the truth. She cried and I knew she was real hurt. She told Dad and he wanted to go over and kill Scott, but I told him, "We love each other; he didn't make me do anything." Then Scott told his folks and they took it bad, too.

A few days later, they came over to our house with Scott so we could talk everything over. It was awful. We were all real stiff and Scott's folks, who used to like me a lot, were, like, cold. Scott and I said we wanted to get married, but my Mom said I was too young and his father said, "No way! Scott's going to college." Then he asked why nobody was talking about an abortion and my folks got real mad.

Pretty soon, we all realized there weren't too many choices. If abortion and marriage were out, I was going to have the baby. I told everyone right then, "I'll raise the baby myself."

Later that night, Scott and I talked on the phone and

we decided we'd wait until I was out of school and 18 and then we'd get married. Our parents couldn't do much about it then.

I was due in August, and I felt real good most of the time. I stayed in school and Scott and I kept on being together, even though our folks would have been happy if we'd split. I think they were afraid we'd run off somewhere.

Most of our friends were great and they didn't treat me any different. But as I got bigger, I noticed that Scott got funny when we were around the other kids. I remember the first time I felt the baby kick. I was real excited and I told Scott! I put his hand on my stomach but he pulled it away fast. I guess he was embarrassed.

After that, he didn't seem as affectionate as he used to be and that hurt me a lot. That was when I really needed him to love me, but he just wasn't the same. He seemed too busy to do a lot of things with me.

A month before school ended, I stopped going to class, but I was able to finish my work at home. I was really tired by that time and I had gotten real self-conscious because I was getting so large. One day, Scott came over and held my hand and told me that he had a great chance to work on a ranch right after graduation—and he was going! I started to cry and I asked him if he still loved me. He said yes, but this was something he really wanted to do and he couldn't pass it up.

I said, "You know, the baby is coming in August." Didn't he want to be there? I remember he waited a long time before he answered, "I just can't make it." I was crushed. I kept thinking it can't be over. But Scott never called and I didn't get invited to his graduation. Why would he want his pregnant girlfriend there to embarrass him? We didn't see each other after that. Scott left for Colorado the week after graduation.

I started getting ready for my baby to come. Mom and I went out and we bought a lot of cute little shirts and nightgowns and booties. When you don't know what sex the baby is, you buy yellow and green instead of pink or blue. A couple of my girlfriends had a shower and they gave me a baby swing and some diapers and a teddy bear and a rattle. My Dad went into the attic and found the crib that all of us kids used and he cleaned it up, and we bought a new mattress for it and some sheets.

I thought about Scott all the time and I kept asking myself, "What happened? Why did he stop loving me?" Was it because I got pregnant and lost his respect for me? Or was I so ugly, with my big belly, that I turned him off? I was really a mess and I cried a lot, even though I got excited as my due date got close.

On August 3rd, three days before I was due, I woke up real early with a backache and a funny feeling in my stomach. I just knew the baby was coming! I woke up everyone and we were all excited. Then I packed a bag with a robe and some makeup, but Mom said I better be patient because I'd probably be in labor for a long time. That's how it is with first children. She was right! I had pains all day, and they got real strong around dinner and that's when we went to the hospital.

That night at 11:18 P.M. my wonderful baby was born! A beautiful little girl! She was 19 inches and weighed seven and a half pounds. I looked at her—she was so beautiful. When they put her in my arms, nothing else mattered, even the fact that Scott wasn't there. I named her Rebecca Lee, but I called her Becky.

While I was in the hospital, a friend of Mom's, Mrs. Carroll, came to see me. She's a counselor in a girls' school. She wanted to know what I was going to do about Becky. I didn't know what she meant, but she started talking about how hard it is to raise a baby alone, without a father. But it didn't bother me at first. I knew my folks would help with Becky when I got a job. I wanted to support the two of us and also finish high school in a special program.

But Mrs. Carroll said, "But what about Becky?" Was it fair to a baby to grow up without a daddy? I just pushed her questions out of my mind. The day I brought Becky home, it was so much fun for all of us! We took turns holding her and feeding her and I kept thinking, I've got enough love for the two of us!

I wish there was a happy ending to this story. I always thought there'd be. But things went bad right from the start. Becky was an adorable little baby, but she was colicky. She screamed every night no matter what we did for her. We'd feed her and hold her and walk around the house with her, and she'd keep on crying. It drove everybody crazy. The doctor said that lots of babies are colicky, that they have gas pains, and it's something they just outgrow. But it really upset all of us; we just couldn't do anything to help her.

I wasn't doing too well either. I had stitches during delivery and they bothered me for a while. But I also was real depressed—baby blues, they call it—and I cried a lot and I missed Scott something fierce. I kept thinking about him, waiting for the phone to ring. I wrote to him and told him about Becky and I was so sure he'd call. I thought maybe he'd come back.

I guess I wasn't too much help with my little baby in that first week or two.

But, worst of all, Mom and Dad kept talking about adoption. Can you believe it? They wanted me to give my baby away! How heartless could they be? Their own grandchild! I know they were thinking of me. They kept saying, "You'll never have a normal life if you raise Becky alone. You won't be able to get an education. You won't be able to have boyfriends and dates and marry a nice boy. No young man wants to get involved with someone else's baby." I didn't want to hear any of it and we had some awful fights.

One night I couldn't sleep. I kept picturing Scott and me and Becky together and we were pushing her in a buggy and everyone was looking at her and saying how darling she was. And I was so happy; Scott and me were in love again. I just kept seeing that picture over and over in my mind. And I was praying and asking God to help make it happen.

The next morning when I woke up I remembered my dream for the three of us. And all of a sudden I knew it was all over, really over. We were never going to be a family. Becky would never have Scott for her daddy. He didn't want either of us. It was like a knife in my heart, thinking that. But I knew it was true. And I didn't really blame him that much. I held little Becky in my arms and I cried for a long time. I told her, "I love you, Baby; I love you and I want you to have a happy life more than anything in the world."

The rest is like a blur. I told Mom that morning that I wanted to talk to someone about finding a couple who would love Becky and be her family. Mom cried and I cried some more and then we told Dad and they made some phone calls. A lady from the adoption agency came over and asked a lot of questions. She said she was sure there were a whole lot of people who would love to have a beautiful little girl like Becky, people who were happily married but who couldn't have children of their own. The lady explained that it would take time to find the best family for her, but that it might be best if they put Becky in a foster home, with a family who took care of little babies while the adoption was being set up.

I was supposed to bring Becky to the adoption agency and they would give her to the foster parents. Eventually, maybe a few months, when they found the right family, I would sign a paper giving up my rights as Becky's mother. But I had to be sure before signing the paper.

I hated it! I almost backed out right then. But the worst time was the day Mom and I got Becky ready to leave us. We dressed her in her best little romper suit and a bonnet and she looked so beautiful. I packed her clothes, all the little things we had bought her, and then we took her to the case worker at the adoption agency.

As I held her for the last time, my heart just tore in half. My baby, this was my baby, and I was giving her away. Mom kept consoling me and my tears kept dropping on Becky's blanket. Mom kept telling me how proud she was that I was putting my baby's happiness first. All I could feel was that I was deserting my baby, giving her to someone who couldn't possibly love her as much as I did.

Becky is gone now. She's now part of a family that's supposed to be real wonderful, and I feel very jealous even though it's what I want. I keep thinking about her little face and her finger curled around mine the last day we had her, and I carry her pictures around wherever I go.

My baby will always be precious to me. I hope that someday her new family will tell her about her first mother. I hope they'll say something like, maybe, "She loved you so much she let us have you because she couldn't give you all you needed. You are lucky you had such a wonderful mommy." Most of all, I hope they love her like I do.

Questions for Reflection/Discussion

1. What part of Kim's story impressed you most? Why?

2. Did she make a good decision about her baby? Why? Why not? What would you have done?

3. How did you feel about Scott's reaction to the pregnancy? Could you understand it? Did he make a good decision? Explain.

4. Who was hurt the most by what happened?

5. How would you have liked the story to end?

~ 22

Last Chance for Questions

Q: Can you get pregnant the first time you have sex?
A: You bet! Don't believe those who say it can't happen.

Q: Is it possible to get pregnant without having sexual intercourse?

A: Yes, absolutely. If a couple gets heavily into petting or "making out," the male may have an ejaculation. If semen is spilled near the woman's vagina, the sperm can swim inside and fertilize an egg which might be there. This is the start of pregnancy.

Q: I know abortion is wrong, but what if the parents don't want the baby. They'll only abuse it after it's born. What kind of life is that?

A: A sad life, but a baby who isn't wanted before birth is often wanted later—by someone. By the time of birth, the parents have usually accepted the baby and are even excited about it. Sometimes, an older couple is shocked when they find out there's a pregnancy, and the baby born to them late in life becomes a most precious gift. On the other hand, a couple may be thrilled with pregnancy but things go wrong after the baby comes—and the wanted child becomes a burden. So, you can see, child abuse doesn't necessarily happen because of a "wanted" or an "unwanted" pregnancy.

Actually, the key factor usually is how the parents themselves were treated as children. A person who was physically or emotionally abused in childhood is most likely to mistreat his or her own child, not because of a lack of love but because we learn how to be parents from our own parents, even though at the time we don't like it.

Q: I pray all the time to do the right thing, but I still do lots of things I shouldn't. Do you think I've got a bad streak?

A: No, I think you've got a "human streak," and by that I mean you're perfectly normal. We all do things we know we shouldn't, no matter how hard we try, since we aren't perfect. Instead of focusing on your failures, why don't you spend a few moments every night thinking of the good things you did that day. Use the sacrament of reconciliation. Keep trying to be your best, but be patient and forgiving of yourself when you fail. Be aware when you do what is good. God understands and loves you.

Q: My feelings get hurt all the time if someone laughs at me, or a guy snubs me, or whatever. Sometimes I cry for no reason at all. Do you think I'm too emotional?

A: I think you're a young woman with lots of tender feelings, and you should bless this gift. As you get older, you will probably be better able to manage your emotions. You also will develop confidence to help you overlook unintended slights.

Q: I made a mistake with a guy—let him go too far—and he never called me again. What can I do to get him back?

A: Why do you want him back? If he really cared about

you, he'd be the one worrying about his behavior. What you may be feeling is shame because you know there wasn't really love between you, yet you gave yourself to him. Now you feel a need to make something out of the relationship so what you did doesn't seem cheap. Accept the fact that you made a mistake and learn from the experience. Ask God's forgiveness. Move on and do better next time. I bet you will.

Q: How come a guy can have sex and still be Mr. Nice Guy, but a girl does it and she's "bad?" Is that fair?

A: No, but it comes out of our old double-standard, where people expected strong morals from women but not from men. It was assumed that men couldn't control their passions, so women were responsible for putting on the brakes. Also, because of their biology, women had to take responsibility for pregnancy when it occurred. A man could walk away without responsibility, unless they were married, and this is still largely true today. Unfair as it is, this reality still influences people's expectations. We need to say, over and over, to young men: You also are responsible for all your sexual behavior.

Q: Is it true that guys can get sick if they don't have sex regularly?

A: Is that old boy's tale still around? Don't believe it! It's just one more variation on a very old theme: "Have sex with me or else." Many men—unmarried, widowed, priests—don't have sex but they are physically and emotionally very healthy.

Q: A bunch of us were fooling around and now I'm afraid I'm pregnant. How can I find out?

A: You can't find out immediately. You may have reason to suspect pregnancy if you are late with your menstrual period. Drugstores have "early pregnancy detection" kits, but these are not foolproof. A medical examination four to six weeks after the pregnancy has begun will give conclusive evidence. You probably know, but just in case you don't, you *cannot* get pregnant from passionate kissing or embracing. Genital contact with ejaculation or, of course, sexual intercourse *can* result in pregnancy. If you find out that you are pregnant, you need to tell your parents, difficult though it will be. In time they will get over the shock and disappointment and will help you through it.

Q: I think I'm the only virgin in my class. I always said I'd wait till marriage. Now I'm beginning to wonder: Is it worth it?

A: Many women who have waited say yes to this question; it's worth it. They know that they avoided the damaging consequences of premarital sex, bringing to their marriage the most special gift a wife or husband can give to the other: one's total self, never before offered to another person.

But how do you know you're the only one not having sex? I'd bet there are many like yourself, feeling pressured to do something because others are talking a lot about their sexual affairs. Don't make decisions that are wrong for you in order to fit in with the crowd. Who says they're right? Be who you are—and be proud of it!

Q: Dad caught a bunch of us watching a porno movie we rented and he made an awful scene. Now my friends aren't welcome at my house and I'm supposed to stay away from them. Is this extreme or what?

A: Sounds like your father reacted strongly out of shock as well as moral principle. Of course, he is right. Films or magazines that degrade persons or show graphic sexual acts and perversions are wrong. It's especially wrong for impressionable young people. Your father doesn't want you to be infected by the poison of pornography, nor to associate with those who like it. Can't blame Dad for that! But maybe you need to talk to him about the punishment. Tell him you're sorry you disappointed him; assure him it won't happen again; speak up for your friends (if they really are friends), and remind him that you're safer at home than anywhere else. Ask him to share his feelings and listen openly to him. Be grateful to have a father who cares enough to discipline!

Q: I get sexual feelings just looking at a guy, at his body. Is this normal for a girl? I'm only 12.

A: I think you're a mature 12, already into puberty and therefore capable of having sexual feelings. Since the feelings are new, your reaction is probably a mix of shock, guilt, pleasure and confusion. Don't dwell on the sights before you and the feelings you get. And don't be alarmed—you'll begin to see the whole person before long, not just the gorgeous hunk!

Q: What is a lesbian?

A: It's a woman who is homosexual.

Q: Is French kissing a sin?

A: French, or "deep," kissing with the tongue involved, is very sexually stimulating. God gives us a physical nature that responds increasingly to sexual stimulus. So, French kissing and other intimate acts are used by married couples as expressions of love and as preparation for total sexual union. They are not appropriate acts for unmarried people and may be sinful if done deliberately to achieve sexual pleasure or to arouse oneself or one's partner to a readiness for intercourse. If you should not have sexual relations, you should not engage in acts that lead to it.

Q: A girl in my class had an abortion. I don't talk to her any more. How could anyone do that to a baby?

A: The challenge for you as Christian is to hate the sin but to love the sinner. This means you may know that a person has done something morally evil. But Jesus tells us that we cannot pass judgment on another person; only God can decide how guilty they are. I would encourage you to be kind to this girl. You don't know what she is feeling inside. You don't know what caused her to do what she did. If she wants to be your friend, be willing to do so, to listen to her. She may need someone like you, a good person, more than ever before in her life.

Q: If sex is so bad, why do people do it?

A: Sex is *not* bad. It is God's gift to human beings. What is bad is how some people use it. Because they are inexperienced, teenagers may get into sex for a lot of reasons that have little to do with committed love. Here is what many teens have said are their reasons:

- to show their parents they are grown up
- to keep a boyfriend (or girlfriend)
- to go along with the crowd
- to get feelings of closeness with someone
- to prove to others they are "normal"
- to prove to themselves they are lovable and attractive
- to get back at someone who has hurt them
- to become popular
- to get pregnant and force a marriage.

These are not good reasons for having sex. The only worthwhile reason for sex is to share and deepen love in the committed relationship of marriage.

Q: Can a girl get AIDS?

A: Yes. Although use of contaminated needles in drug use and male homosexual activity are the most common causes of AIDS, a growing number of men and women who don't use drug needles and are not homosexual are becoming infected with the AIDS virus. If a girl has sex with a guy who has had sex with an AIDS carrier, she too can become infected. Those at risk include any and all persons involved in casual sex.

Q: What if I get married and can't have children?

A: There is that chance—one couple in eight cannot bear children. Many young couples put off having a baby, without knowing whether they can have one or not. When they finally try, they find out that one of them is not fertile. Sometimes doctors are able to treat sterility and help a couple achieve pregnancy. If this doesn't happen, they may seek to adopt a baby. The problem is that there are very few newborn white infants available because of abortion and because many unmarried women choose to raise their own child. Sometimes couples adopt and lovingly raise children who are older, of mixed races, or who have some health problem or handicap. Others decide to channel their needs and interests into other worthwhile activities.

Q: Don't you think living together is a good way for a couple to test their love?

A: On the contrary, it often is the worst way. Couples who have tried it admit that it really isn't like marriage because they don't feel secure with each other. After all, there have been no vows, no expressed public commitment to each other. So they tend to put on their good side only, to avoid discussion on issues that might cause arguments. They really don't get to know each other very well. Also, when they live together, the pressure builds to marry, even if one or both of them realize they aren't suited to each other. The pressure may come from inside or from one another: "After all, I've given my best to you." Vows said later under such pressure are more easily discarded. In fact, a study by the National Bureau of Economic Research found that couples who lived together before marriage had "nearly an 80 percent higher divorce rate than those who did not...." Of course, living together before marriage also is morally wrong. Therefore it's a poor basis for a happy Christian marriage.

Q: Can a guy stay a virgin?

A: Why not? Lots of them do. There is absolutely nothing mandatory about sex. Men don't get ill or crazy if they don't have it. Of course, given our cultural emphasis, many men feel they must be sexually active, even if they don't feel ready. Often, just as girls do, guys give in to the pressure.

Q: I don't care about a career or an education. I just want to get married and have kids. What's wrong with that?

A: Absolutely nothing. Millions of women have remained at home and raised children and loved it (I'm one of them). Just be sure that you don't short-circuit your development. Don't rush into a marriage while you're still very young; those marriages seldom succeed. Don't short-cut your education. God has given you certain talents and gifts and you need to develop these. Further, you probably will want (and need) to work at various times in your life: before marriage, to help with kids' college costs, after they leave home, etc. Creating a home of love and a family of joy together with your husband is a marvelous vocation. But it is no longer the whole of life for most of us.

~ 23

A Dream for the Future

Life now is full and exciting and your adult future seems far away. That's fine. We each need to live fully in the present moment. But I can't resist offering just a few more ideas for those days and years that are ahead of you.

Most of you, I'm sure, look forward to a happy marriage and family life. Of course, no one can predict or guarantee that this will happen. But if you do marry some day, here are several factors that will influence your chance for happiness as a married person.

1. Age Don't marry too young. Admittedly, there are some people who are happily wed to their childhood sweetheart. But you have more likelihood of success if you wait until your middle or late twenties or even later to say "I do." Marriage is not for children. It is hard work, especially in the first five years or so. There will be many differences to work out. You will need to come to know one another on a deeper level, to become more patient and forgiving, to compromise when there is conflict (and there will be conflict). Such adjustments demand maturity and self-discipline, and most people haven't achieved these qualities early in life (nor some of us even in our fifties!).

Age is important, also, because youthful personalities are in great flux; they grow and develop and evolve, and this is good. Someone whom you dearly love at 19 may radically change by 25, and so will you! If you marry at 20, by 30 you and your husband may be two different people, perhaps not at all suited to each other. I see this happen frequently, and it's tragic when two good persons divorce because they got together too early.

2. Common Values Young people are often attracted to those who are quite different from themselves. There is an attraction to even the strange and bizarre person! But your best foundation for marriage lies in finding someone with a similar background, someone who shares many of the same goals and ideals, who worships God as you do, whose family values are not too unlike your own. Even strong personality differences can cause difficulties. If you're a dreamer, a bookworm, a would-be artist, and you marry a young man who thinks Saturday Night Live and Sunday afternoon football are the ultimate, you may bore one another to tears. If you aren't sure motherhood is worth sacrificing for, and your future husband dreams of a houseful of kids, conflict is inevitable. Don't compromise on cherished values and beliefs, no matter how much in love you may be.

3. Communication You may think right now that the "strong, silent type" is fascinating. But proceed cautiously before marrying him, unless you uncover lots of warmth, feelings, and ideas behind his quiet exterior. Talking, you will discover, is the life-blood of marriage. Without it, you will never have a really intimate relationship. It is not enough for you to be a big talker, very open with your feelings and your dreams. To live the good life together, dialogue must be a two-way street. Without it, you will be lonely. And don't believe that a man who doesn't want to talk things over and who gives you the silent treatment before marriage will change afterward. He will only become more private and silent—and you, more frustrated.

4. Realism As they say "I do," many young couples have highly unrealistic expectations for marriage. Through rose-colored glasses, they see their beloved as a hero or a perfect creature. They expect total fulfillment at the hands of this person. Marriage will solve their problems and put an end to loneliness, they believe. Because they're marrying the one they love, marriage will be easy—no sweat!

This is all a perfect dream, but it isn't real! None of us is perfect; no love can be without pain; human loneliness ends only when we are finally united with God. So start out by knowing that happy marriage won't be easy to achieve; at times it will be very tough. Unless you know this, you may come to blame each other or think you each have married the wrong person.

5. Character Physical beauty enchants us, but spiritual beauty means more and lasts longer. It isn't enough to "love" the person you marry. You also need to like him, to admire and respect him, to see in his heart the qualities that make him friend as well as lover.

As my four daughters grew up, my mother often told them about why she married their grandfather. Mom had seven proposals of marriage. Each time, she asked herself this question: "Would I be proud to call him the father of my children?" For her, this meant: Is he a person of dignity and character, someone who is kind and honorable, someone I can look at and admire? "I was in love each time and I tried to say yes," explained Mom to my daughters, "but each time the answer was no!" Finally, when she was almost 30, Dad came along. She finally could answer her own question: "yes," and the answer to my Dad's question became a "yes" as well. They had a wonderful marriage that lasted 42 years until death separated them.

6. Faith There used to be a book called *Three to Get Mar-*

ried. It was about the role that God plays in our lives as married people. It explained that when you make your vows as a Christian couple, God is the third person in your marriage, providing you with grace all along the way. All you have to do is ask for God's help. I believe this because it's been true in my own marriage. I don't believe that my husband, Ray, and I would still be married unless God had been very much a part of our life together, on good days and during difficult times.

God, who made each of us male or female, also intended for us to live together and to love and care for each other. So when you begin to look toward getting married, know that God will help you to choose a good man and to find joy and happiness with him.

7. Children Some people think a family is not very important any more. You may know young couples who feel this way. They probably have been influenced by societal voices which tell them that children cost a lot of money and take away all their privacy and freedom. Well, there's a certain truth to that: kids do cost lots of money to clothe, feed, educate, and keep in pocket money! Children use up a lot of energy from the time they're tiny babies who need feeding and changing through the teen years when the struggle of wills wears out even the most vigorous parent! Maybe you've already heard something like this from your folks.

Children also may cause parents grief and worry. The reason, of course, is that they *love* them! And when kids get sick or have problems or take the wrong path, parents suffer right along with the kids. Children disappoint their parents too, and sometimes they hurt them by pulling away from their love. This isn't because teenagers are bad; they just need to break out of the tight bonds of parental love and can be thoughtless in doing this.

Parents sacrifice and struggle and for many years; they don't know if they are being good parents, if they are raising their children to be loving and happy people. Sometimes the question isn't answered until the parents are very old. Is it any wonder some people don't think they want to be a mother or father?

But I encourage you and challenge you to take that risk someday. If you accept this risk to become a parent—and God blesses that willingness—you will experience love that you never imagined! You will look down at that little creature, born of the love between you and your spouse, and you will be filled with awe and wonder and your heart will overflow with joy. Life will be brighter and so precious because each day you share the beauty and the struggle with children you love more than your own life.

I wish you great happiness as you grow into womanhood and accept the challenges that adult life brings. May your days be filled with joy and the love of good people. May God embrace you forever.

To the Parents,

Someone once said that an adolescent is a person with one foot in childhood's garden and the other tenaciously planted on adult turf.

Indeed, adolescence is a period of transition and transformation during which the emerging young adult struggles with emotional, spiritual, mental, and physical change. Small wonder that teenagers need all the love and patience we can muster.

Up to this time, life for them has been fairly uncomplicated. From birth on, the child builds a self-image, a montage of beliefs about himself or herself based on what "significant others" (mostly parents) suggest: We love you. You are a valuable person. Or, for some children, opposite messages. The child's self-concept is also impacted by other family members, a growing circle of outsiders, and by life's challenges and opportunities.

Uncritically, the child accepts the beliefs and practices of parents. But as adolescence arrives, the values "learned" in the family may no longer satisfy the teenager. Instead, the young person begins to reach toward identity and to seek convictions that truly are his or her own.

This is so right, for the fundamental task of the adolescent is ultimately to separate from parents, to discover and develop an individual identity, to find his or her unique self. Ultimately, adolescence is preparation for moving out into the world as a new creation.

It becomes clear to 14-year-old Charlie that he no longer can be just Jim and Mary King's oldest son. At 13, Dawn becomes unwilling to be identified merely as the O'Brien "baby." Each begins to examine the question directly: Who am I? What am I here for? What can I really be?

In this process, most teenagers rebel over relatively minor issues: house rules, choice of friends, clothing, makeup, what foods they will eat, and—to parental consternation—whether Sunday Mass is for them!

Some adolescents, spurred by their growing intellectual powers of abstract thinking and reasoning, are bold enough to challenge parental wisdom. Fired with idealism, they may enjoy pointing out contradictions in what parents say and actually do. Arguments about any and all subjects satisfy the need, at some level, to reject parents and to test new-found ideas and convictions. Such revolt is the normal way for teens to assert their own will. Parents are fortunate if their teenagers don't involve themselves in more damaging behavior, such as drinking, drugs, or irresponsible sexual activity.

Strong emotions also are a component of this newly forming person. If you live with a teenager, I don't need to elaborate on the wide mood swings, the exhilarating highs and painful lows that occur with little warning. Teens are great, good fun to have around when they're "up," but deep feelings of insecurity, sensitivity, loneliness, and fear of failure can cause even the sunniest teen to plummet to the depths.

Most such moods are usually over as quickly as they come. But parents and those who work with adolescents need to be alert to persistent depression as a possible warning sign of deeper emotional disturbance. Support and sometimes counseling can help a teen weather these times.

Emotional turmoil and intellectual ferment is complicated by the physical changes of puberty. Sexual maturation today occurs as young as 10 years of age in girls and 12 years in boys. Young bodies grow and change in mysterious ways that the youngsters don't understand. The early developers are self-conscious and embarrassed; the late bloomers anxious and embarrassed. And all of them wonder: Am I normal? Is something wrong with me?

Along with physical development comes, unbidden, sexual feelings and urges and great curiosity, which may generate strong guilt feelings. It can make the child extremely vulnerable to equally uninformed peers and to the commercial purveyers of explicit sex and sexual titillation.

By trial and error, confusion and insight, the young teens should gradually come to accept their sexuality as normal, even joyful. The goal is to integrate their sexual nature into their total personality, to cope with scary though fascinating encounters with the other sex, and to develop Christian values which lead to moral decisions.

Many mothers and fathers are baffled why their children don't simply conform to traditional values, the values that they, the parents, embraced. Such parents tend to overlook the culture their offspring are living in, one that bombards them with stimulating sexual images and other, often subliminal, messages.

By and large, the mass media projects a central sexual theme: anything goes. Explicit love scenes, adultery, sexual violence, homosexuality, incest, and nudity are common movie and television fare. Films rated "R" and "PG" idealize sexual freedom and suggest that all normal persons are sexually active, no matter what their state in life. Soft porn movies and videocassettes are available to all. Rock musicians and sports heroes blatantly model a sex/drugs/pleasure lifestyle, projecting the message: If it feels good, do it.

Changed social mores intensify the pressure: boy–girl parties, single dating at 12 or 13, deep involvement at 16, the privacy of cars and homes without adults present, easy access to alcohol, drugs, and contraceptives—all contribute to the situation.

Sadly, even so-called responsible adults in government

and education proclaim that teenage chastity is impossible, that contraceptives and abortion protect the young from the "inevitable," damaging consequences of sexual behavior.

Meanwhile, our young teenagers try to sort it all out. What does it mean to be a sexual person? How can I be sexy? Is sex before marriage wrong? Why? How can I say no?

Is it any wonder that a million adolescent girls become pregnant each year in this country? That 400,000 of them will have abortions? That hundreds of thousands of kids decide to do the "honorable thing" and marry, shortcircuiting their future and, in the great majority of cases, ending up in the divorce court? Is it surprising that venereal disease rates continue at epidemic rates? That teens succumb to the pressures and temptations all around them?

What, if anything, can parents do? How can you create a climate in which your son or daughter can build strong values that reject the false messages coming from the culture? Four suggestions come to mind.

1. Provide a home environment of openness, honesty, and compassion. Here, ideas and differences can be talked about with mutual respect; real feelings and fears can be shared. Most parents I know want such a climate in their home.

But when the teen years arrive, parents are afraid to hear what their children are really thinking about and experiencing. They want what's best for the kids, but they fear the worst: Jimmy or Joanne is engaged in dangerous behavior. The real problem is that they don't know how to stop it. Confronting the issue is so painful and—perhaps—futile. So they permit a wall of silence to build up between the children and themselves, depriving the teens of counsel when they most need it.

2. Offer healthy role models. Adolescents need to be around adults who believe it is good to be a man or woman, who find, in all dimensions of their lives, fulfillment in being sexual persons.

Priests, nuns, and brothers, who appreciate their sexuality as men and women, despite their celibate lifestyle, can offer a wonderful example to youth, especially when present in the home as friends. Teens need to be around adults who live by principles of faith, fidelity and honor, people who are willing to be vulnerable enough to share their deepest beliefs and the reasons why they believe as they do. As parents, you offer a real gift when you share what life has taught you, when you express convictions based on your experience. Too often, we parents lay down principles and abstract arguments, and fail to convey the human reality behind our beliefs.

3. Help your child to develop and maintain high self-esteem. Even the most loved and confident child can lose a strong self-image during adolescence. A most significant way to bolster a child's sagging confidence is to express, often and consistently, that he or she is okay in spite of conflict and failure. Teens need to hear that it's a great thing to grow up. They especially should know they are loved for what they are, not merely for what they do.

Helping adolescents to develop positive feelings about themselves strengthens their power to make good decisions. Teens who don't like or trust themselves become pawns in the hands of others. What Dorothy Corkville Briggs expresses here of a boy applies to your daughter as well.

> The stronger the youngster's sense of personal worth the more secure he feels in a group, the easier it is for him to base his decisions on personal conviction rather than on the need for group approval. The lower his self-respect, the less he belongs, the stronger the temptation to go along with group pressures to win a place for himself.

Young girls in our culture especially need to be encouraged to believe in the importance of their intellectual and personal growth and not to be afraid to excel or succeed. As girls reach their mid-teens, they too often bury their gifts in a quest for acceptance from their peers and from society at large.

4. Offer a Christian vision of sexuality. If you were raised in a home where sex was a dirty word, you may find it difficult to talk openly. You may find it hard to face up to your teen's emerging sexuality, and to acknowledge your own. You may feel unsure and ill-prepared to deal with the topic of sex.

But consider this: if you say nothing, from whom will your son or daughter learn? Is there anyone with greater interest in your child than you? Is there anyone more than you who wants what's best for her? Who knows this child better than you do? And, after all, *you* are a sexual being with a lifetime of sexual living, including an intimate sexual relationship and bearing and bringing new human life into existence.

So instead of holding back, I would encourage you to speak simply but bravely, honestly but humbly to your teenager, offering a Christian vision of what being a man or being a woman has meant to you. No written text can replace this gift which you can offer your daughter at this momentous moment in her life.

My hope is that this book can provide information and some new insights but, more importantly, can foster between you and your youngster deeper levels of sharing and trust on an issue that is at the heart of our humanness.

Bibliography

For Girls

Have You Hugged Your Family Today? A Young Christian Book for Girls, Barbara DeGrote-Sorensen, Augsburg, Minneapolis, 1987, $4.95.

I'm Not the Same Person I Was Yesterday, Jay C. Rochelle, Fortress Press, Philadelphia, 1974, $4.95.

Letters to Teens, Archbishop Rembert G. Weakland, O.S.B., Liguori Publications, Liguori, Mo., 1989, $1.50.

Lord, Do You Hear Me? Sr. Maureen Skelly, S.C.H., ed., Regina Press, New York, 1986, $4.95.

Sex, Love or Infatuation: How Can I Really Know? Ray Short, Augsburg, Minneapolis, 1978, $4.50.

10 Tough Issues for Teenagers, Jim Auer, Liguori Publications, Liguori, Mo., 1989, $1.95.

Understanding Sex and Sexuality, Nancy Hennessy Cooney, Wm. C. Brown Company, Dubuque, Iowa, 1987.

For Parents

Adolescence: What's a Parent to Do? Richard D. Parsons, Paulist Press, Mahwah, N.J., $5.95.

Helping Your Teenager, Len Kageler, Christian Publications, $9.95.

Ministry of Parents to Teenagers, Simeon J. Thole, O.S.B., Liturgical Press, Collegeville, Minn., 1985, $1.25.

Parents Talk Love: The Catholic Family Handbook About Sexuality, Susan K. Sullivan, Matthew A. Kawiak, Paulist Press, Mahwah, N.J., 1984, $7.95.

The Quicksilver Years: The Hopes and Fears of Early Adolescence, Peter Benson, Dorothy Williams, Arthur Johnson, Harper & Row, New York, $13.95.

A Sense of Sexuality, Christian Love and Intmacy, Evelyn Eaton Whitehead & James D. Whitehead, Doubleday, New York, N.Y., 1989, $16.95.

Sex Education for Toddlers to Young Adults: A Guide for Parents, James Kenny, St. Anthony Messenger Press, Cincinnati, 1989, $4.25.

Glossary

Abortion - The premature termination of pregnancy. Voluntary abortion is one done at the request of the mother. Spontaneous abortion, called a miscarriage, is a natural termination of pregnancy due to some abnormal development of the fetus.

Abstinence - Voluntarily refraining from sexual intercourse.

Adolescence - The period of time during which the boy or girl leaves childhood and develops the physical, mental, and spiritual tools to live as an adult.

Adultery - Sexual relations between two people, one or both of whom are married to someone else.

Amenorrhea - The medical name for a missed menstrual period.

Amniocentesis - A procedure in which a sample of fluid surrounding the fetus is drawn and analyzed to detect possible birth defects.

Androgen - A substance that influences the growth and sex drive in the male and produces masculine secondary characteristics (e.g. voice, hair, growth, etc.).

Anus - The opening between the buttocks at the lower end of the large intestine, from which waste matter is expelled.

Birth control - Prevention of birth by any method, including contraception, sterilization, or abortion.

Bisexual - A person equally attracted to males and females and may have sex with either.

Breech birth - The birth position of the baby, feet or bottom first, instead of the usual head-first position.

Buttocks - The part of the body you sit down on. The "backside" or "behind."

Caesarean section - A surgical incision (cutting through the abdomen into the uterus) to deliver the baby when normal delivery is difficult.

Castration - The removal of the testicles in males or the ovaries in females.

Cervix - The narrow neck or entrance into the woman's uterus (womb).

Chastity - The proper use of sex; for example, refraining from sexual relations when not married, or, if married, having sex only with one's spouse.

Chromosome - The thread-like material in the egg and sperm that contain the genes.

Circumcision - Cutting away the loose skin, called the foreskin, around the tip of the male penis.

Climax - See Orgasm.

Clitoris - A small and sensitive penis-like organ of the female located within the vagina. The seat of sexual stimulation.

Coitus - Another name for sexual intercourse.

Conception - The beginning of a new life in the womb, when egg and sperm join.

Condom - A rubber or latex sheath (like a rubber balloon) placed over the penis in order to catch the sperm before it gets into the vagina. A contraceptive, but may also be used to prevent sexually transmitted disease.

Contraception - Various methods that prevent conception (contra=against, ception=conceive).

Contraceptives - Any means to prevent birth by keeping the sperm and egg from meeting: drugs, condoms, devices, pills, etc.

Cunnilingus - Applying one's mouth or tongue to the genitals in order to sexually stimulate the female. (One form of oral sex.)

Douche - The cleansing of the vagina with a stream of liquid solution or water.

Dysmenorrhea - Medical term for cramping or other discomfort during menstruation.

Ejaculation - The discharge of the seed fluid, or semen, from the penis. Having a male orgasm.

Embryo - The new life in the mother's womb, up to eight weeks.

Erection - The enlargement and stiffening of the penis as its tissues fill with blood.

Erotic - Sexually stimulating.

Estrogen - A hormone that affects the female cycle and secondary sex characteristics (breast development, hair, growth, etc.).

Fallopian tube - The tube through which the egg passes on its way to the uterus.

Fellatio - Applying the mouth to the penis to sexually stimulate the male (another form of oral sex).

Fertilization - The entrance of the male sperm into the female egg.

Fetus - A name given the unborn baby from the third month in the mother's womb till birth.

Foreplay - The touches, kisses, etc. before intercourse to get each other ready.

Fornication - Sexual intercourse between an unmarried man and an umarried woman.

Foreskin - The skin covering the glans, or tip of the penis; often cut away by circumcision.

Gene - The unit of heredity.

Genitalia - The external sex organs.

Glans - The very tip or head of the penis.

Heterosexual - One who is sexually attracted to and/or active with persons of the opposite sex.

Homosexual - One who is sexually attracted to and/or active with persons of the same sex.

Hysterectomy - Surgical removal of the uterus.

Illegitimate - Refers to a child born of parents who are not married.

Impotence - The inability of the male to have or maintain an erection during sexual intercourse.

Intercourse, sexual - The insertion of the male penis into the female vagina.

Lesbian - A female homosexual.

Masturbation - Stimulating one's sexual organs, often to the point of orgasm.

Menopause - The end of the ovulation and menstruation cycle in women, usually between the ages of 45 and 55. Also called a change of life or climacteric.

Menstruation - The monthly flow of blood from the uterus, usually occurring every 28-30 days; the monthly period, having a period.

Nocturnal emission - The involuntary discharge of the extra, stored-up semen at night during sleep, sometimes in connection with a "sexy" dream. Also called a wet dream.

Obstetrics and gynecology (OB-GYN) - Medical specialty that treats women in pregnancy or for female reproductive problems.
Oral sex - See Cunnilingus and Fellatio.
Orgasm - The peak of sexual excitement; for the male it is the spurting out of the semen from the penis; for the female, an overall body glow and relaxation.
Ovaries - The two female sex glands in which eggs are formed.
Ovulation - The release of a ripe egg into the Fallopian tube.
Ovum - The female egg (plural: ova).
Pap smear - Procedure to test for cancer, involving a scraping of cells from the vagina and cervix.
Pelvic exam - Routine exam doctors do to check for any abnormalities of a woman's reproductive organs.
Penis - The male, finger-like sex organ through which semen is discharged and urine is passed.
Pituitary gland - The "master gland" in the brain's "control center" that controls the functions of all the other glands, especially the sex glands.
Placenta - Sometimes called the afterbirth. This is the sponge-like organ that connects the fetus to the lining of the mother's uterus by means of the umbilical cord. It serves to exchange air, food, and waste matter between the mother to the fetus.
Procreation - Literally "to create for" God; to beget children as a delegate for God.
Prophylactic - Another term for condom.
Prostitute - One who has sex for money.
Puberty - The start of adolescence.
Pubic hair - The course hair that grows around the sexual organs usually in a triangular patch.
Rape - Forcible sexual intercourse against another's consent.
Rectum - See Anus.
Safe period - The interval in the female menstrual cycle when no ripe egg is present in the system and therefore she is unable to become pregnant.
Scrotum - The thick sac of skin between the male's legs containing the testicles.
Semen - Also called the seed or seed fluid or seminal fluid. It is

made up of the life-giving male sperm and is ejaculated or spurted through the penis when the male reaches an orgasm.

Sexuality - The state of being a sexual person all over and all the time. One's personality given push and dimension by sex. A person's all-over "posture" in life as a male or female.

Shaft - The long, finger-like part of the male sex organ; that part of the penis as distinct from the tip or head (called the glans).

Sodomy - Inserting the penis into the rectum.

Sperm - The male reproductive cell.

STD (Sexually Transmitted Disease) - See Venereal Disease.

Sterility - The inability to reproduce.

Testicles - Also called testes (slang: "balls," "nuts," etc.). The two male sex glands within the scrotum sac which produce the sperm.

Tubal ligation - Cutting and tying the ends of a woman's fallopian tubes so that the egg can't get through. A form of sterilization.

Transsexual - One who undergoes surgery to obtain the outward appearance of the other sex.

Transvestite - One who has a compulsion to dress up in the clothes of the opposite sex.

Umbilical cord - The tube between the mother's placenta and the baby.

Urine - The liquid waste matter.

Uterus - Also called the womb. The small, pear-shaped organ of the female in which the baby develops.

Vagina - Also called the birth canal. The opening between the women's legs, between the uterus and the vulva, which receives the male penis and also through which the baby passes at birth.

Vasectomy - The duct that carries the male sperm is cut and tied. A form of male sterilization.

Venereal disease - Any of the variety of contagious sexual diseases. Also referred to as the STDs (Sexually Transmitted Diseases), such as genital herpes, syphilis, gonorrhea, AIDS, etc.

Virgin - One who has never had sexual intercourse.

Vulva - The female outside sexual organs, the two mounds that lead to the vagina and clitoris.

Wet dream - See Nocturnal emission.

Womb - See Uterus.

Health Hints
Spiritual and Physical

At the turn of the century psychologists and psychiatrists used to describe adolescence as the time of great "storm and stress," wild mood swings, inner turmoil, and risky behavior. Well, we know now that they oversold their case. In fact, in making such a general statement, they were wrong. As we saw in the book, the large majority of adolescents (some scientists say 80 percent)—yes, with a few battles here and there—make the transition from child to adult with fairly good grace and with good relationships with their parents.

One thing, unfortunately, hasn't changed, the one thing you think would: the death rate for teenagers. And what is mind-blowing are the causes. In the old days (back at the turn of the century and earlier and even right up to the 1940s and 1950s) teenagers died for medical reasons, that is, from diseases we have since overcome with immunization and antibiotics. So what are teenagers dying from these days? From "social" diseases: accidents, suicides, homicides, drug and alcohol abuse, and the STDs. The latest statistic is that 77 percent of those deaths for 15- to 24-year-olds are attributed to accident, suicide, and homicide. Moreover, teens' future health is much threatened by the habits they're forming now: smoking, alcohol, drug abuse, lack of exercise, and poor nutrition. Usually these victims are in that 20 percent who don't go through adolescence very well.

Anyway, here's a little health chart that gives you the most common areas that a teenager ought to see a doctor about in a normal routine checkup—and a priest or any adult he or she trusts for the rest.

AREA OF CONCERN	SUGGESTION
Ears: The loud music you sometimes listen to, especially through head-phones, has damaged the hearing of millions.	You should have your hearing tested in early adolescence (maybe 13, 14) and late adolescence (say 18, 19). Plan to take a few days retreat or go on a "Search" weekend. Quiet reflective prayerful times are necessary to grow and learn to listen for God's voice.
Eyes: It is estimated that about one in four teenag-ers needs some vision correction, especially those who spend a lot of time at computers or TV.	Here you should be screened every year or two. Learn to really see nature which is always healing.
Teeth: Gum disease, tooth decay, and a bad bite are common among teenagers.	To the dentist twice a year!

AREA OF CONCERN	SUGGESTION
Emotions: All the changes and challenges of teenagers can be hard. You feel like you're starting over and may have to give up a lot, including emotional security. This may cause depression.	Talk to a trusted friend, confide in a parent, pray. See your school counselor, who understands the stresses and problems of teenagers.
Blood, Missed Periods: Anemia, a shortage of iron in the blood, is fairly common in adolescence. So, too, are delayed or missed menstrual periods.	You need plenty of protein and iron in your diet. Try beans, eggs, milk, lean meat. Stress can be a factor too. Go easy.
Sex Organs, STD'S: Menstrual problems may require a doctor's attention. External and internal sex organs as well as breasts need to be examined periodically for cancer.	A family doctor or OB-GYN will do a pelvic exam to check for rash, signs of infection, other abnormalities. You can learn to check your breasts for possible lumps.

AREA OF CONCERN	SUGGESTION
Spine: Scoliosis, or curvature of the spine, affects many teens. More common are back problems and poor posture.	Ask your health teacher to check for scoliosis, which can be cured if caught early enough. Too much TV, slumped in a chair, causes back pain. Try walking, regular exercise for health and beauty!
Drugs, alcohol, and smoking: These are current killers. Think of people you know or celebrities and sports figures who are dead from them. To you, these are future killers or disablers and the future seems far off. But the pressures are great.	No hard-sell facts or figures, no videotapes of dead bodies or drug war shoot-outs or the role of organized crime, of the teens in mental hospitals damaged from crack is likely to dissuade the teenager who smokes, drinks, or takes drugs. Only a better vision of oneself and the conviction of God's love can do that. Prayer, going to church, faith are called for here.

Index

Toll-Free Hotline Numbers

Counselling and information are available at these national toll-free numbers:

Covenant House 1-800-999-9999
National Problem Pregnancy Hotline 1-800-228-0332
Lifeline Crisis Pregnancy Hotline 1-800-852-LOVE
Birthright 1-800-848-LOVE
Bethany Christian Services 1-800-BET-HANY
The Pearson Foundation Pregnancy Hotline 1-800-392-2121
Child (Physical or Sexual) Abuse Hotline 1-800-422-4453
AIDS Hotline 1-800-342-AIDS
V.D. (or STD) Hotline 1-800-227-8922
National Cocaine Hotline 1-800-COC-AINE
National Runaway Switchboard 1-800-621-4000 or 1-800-231-6946
Suicide Hotline - call INFOLINE
Alcohol Hotline 1-800-NCA-CALL

For free short-term *Volunteers Catalog* for youth interested in the various ministries in the church, either at home or abroad, write to:
The National Federation for Catholic Youth Ministry
3025 Fourth Street, NE
Washington, D.C. 20017